Homeowner SURVIVAL GUIDE

LANDSCAPING

LANDSCAPING

The DIY Guide to Planning, Planting, and Building a Better Yard

Homeowner SURVIVAL GUIDE

Distributed By
Fox Chapel Publishing

FOX CHAPEL
PUBLISHING

© 2012 by Skills Institute Press LLC
"Homeowner Survival Guide" series trademark of Skills Institute Press
Published and distributed in North America by Fox Chapel Publishing Company, Inc., 1970 Broad Street, East Petersburg, PA.

Landscaping is an original work, first published in 2012.

Portions of text and artwork previously published by and reproduced under license with Direct Holdings Americas Inc.

ISBN 978-1-56523-699-8

Library of Congress Cataloging-in-Publication Data

Landscaping. -- 1st ed.
    p. cm. -- (Homeowner survival guide)
  Includes index.
  "Skills Institute Press."
  ISBN 978-1-56523-699-8
  1. Landscape gardening. 2. Gardens--Design. I. Fox Chapel Publishing. II. Skills Institute Press. III. Series: Homeowner survival guide.
  SB473.L36932 2012
  635.9--dc23
                        2011041874

To learn more about the other great books from Fox Chapel Publishing, or to find a retailer near you,
call toll-free 800-457-9112 or visit us at *www.FoxChapelPublishing.com*.

Note to Authors: We are always looking for talented authors to write new books . Please send a brief letter
describing your idea to Acquisition Editor, 1970 Broad Street, East Petersburg, PA 17520.

Printed in China
First printing

Table of Contents

What You Can Learn

CHAPTER 4
Patios of Brick and Concrete,
Adding a patio or even tile stepping stones will make your landscape more useable by the whole family.

CHAPTER 5
Fences and Walls,
Fences and walls can add privacy and structure to any outdoor location.

CHAPTER 6
The Finishing Touches,
With everything else in place, adding brightly colored flowers or a beautiful trellis can finish off a landscape.

CHAPTER 1

Plans and Preliminaries

Whether you are considering planting a single shrub or remaking your entire yard, successful landscaping begins with a well-thought-out plan. Besides forecasting results, it can show where improvements need to be made. Then, armed with the proper tools, you can level uneven ground, grade or terrace slopes, correct faulty drainage, and enrich soil in preparation for making your landscaping plan a reality.

Planning and working the soil are both important parts of proper preparation.

Caring for Landscaping Tools

A collection of gardening equipment represents a big investment and should be treated accordingly. Proper storage and maintenance will prolong the life of your tools. Moreover, simple repairs can often restore broken or aging equipment to full usefulness.

BASIC CARE

Tools should be kept indoors in a place free of rust-producing moisture; before putting them away, clean them and wipe them dry. Protect cutting tools against corrosion with a light application of household oil. Sharpen blades when they become dull. Carefully clean chemical sprayers after each use.

EASY REPAIRS

Typical troubles with a garden hose are treatable through surgery. If the hose develops a leak, remove the damaged section and make a splice with a mending kit; if a coupling is corroded or loose, cut it off and clamp a new one in place *(page 12)*. A tool with a broken handle can also be salvaged in almost all cases; replacement handles are generally available.

On shovels, rakes, hoes, and other lightweight garden tools, the new handle slides into a metal sleeve and is fastened with screws. The heads of heavy tools such as axes, sledgehammers, and mattocks have a collar that accommodates a thicker handle, and the repair also involves some extra steps *(page 14)*.

CAUTION

DISCONNECT IGNITION WIRE FIRST
Before removing a lawnmower blade to sharpen it, be sure to disconnect the motor's ignition wire from the spark plug to prevent inadvertent starting.

HANDLING CHEMICALS SAFELY
When cleaning sprayers, dump all rinse water into a separate container. Wrap paper around any wire and swabs used in the cleaning. Take the waste materials to your area's toxic waste pickup or disposal facility. Do not pour chemical wastes down the drain.

TOOLS

- Electric drill
- Flat file
- Grinding stone drill attachment
- Hammer
- Knife
- Screwdriver
- Small sledgehammer
- Whetstone

SAFETY TIP

Wear gloves when cleaning any part of a sprayer, and wear goggles when sharpening metal blades and when hammering tool heads onto new handles.

SHARPENING PRUNING SHEARS AND MOWER BLADES

Honing a pair of shears

Disassemble the shears by removing the hinge bolt. Put a few drops of light household oil or water on a whetstone's coarse side. Hold the beveled edge of the blade flush against the stone *(right)* and, starting at the tip, grind in small circles until the blade's edge is keen. Smooth the beveled edge by honing it on the whetstone's fine side with the same grinding motion. Reassemble the shears. You can also use a flat file *(photograph)* to sharpen shears: File the blade as described below for a lawnmower blade.

Coarse Grain

Fine Grain

Flate File

Grinding Stone

Nylon Guide

Beveled Edge

Flat File

A keen edge for a lawnmower blade

Secure the blade in a vise. Lay a flat file flush with the beveled cutting edge *(left)*, and file in the direction indicated by the arrow; do not pull back. File evenly along the whole edge. When the edge looks shiny, file the burr off the underside. Sharpen the blade's other end the same way. Check for balance by hanging the blade on a nail sticking horizontally out of your workbench. If one end is heavier, sharpen it until the blade balances. To use a grinding stone drill attachment, place the nylon guide against the blade's underside *(inset)*. Turn on the drill and, holding the stone against the beveled edge, move it back and forth until the blade is sharp.

MENDING A HOSE

A splice to fix a leak

Cut out the leaking section of the hose. Soak the cut ends in hot water to soften the vinyl. Slip a lock nut from the mending kit over one cut end, with the nut's threads facing out toward the cut. Put a ring over the same end, then push the connector into the hose as far as it can go *(above)*. Slide the lock nut over the ring, and tighten the nut securely to the connector by hand. Repeat on the other end of the hose.

A new coupling for a hose end

Cut off the defective coupling. Push the new coupling into the cut end of the hose as far as it will go. Place the clamp halves around the hose at the base of the coupling, and screw the halves together to tighten the clamp *(right)*.

FLUSHING OUT A GARDEN-HOSE SPRAYER

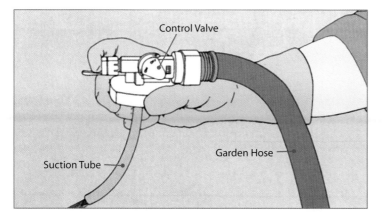

Control Valve

Suction Tube

Garden Hose

Back-flushing the sprayer head
Remove the container from the sprayer head, leaving the head attached to the garden hose. Turn the control valve of the sprayer to ON, and cover the outlet hole with a finger *(left)*. Run water through the hose; the water will flush back through the sprayer and out of the suction tube, washing away chemical residues. Catch the water and residues in a separate container. Remove your finger from the outlet hole, and run water through the sprayer in the normal direction; if the hole is clogged, clear it with stiff wire.

KEEPING A CANISTER SPRAYER CLEAN

Spray-Directing Tube

Pistol Grip

Nozzle

Canister

Hose

O-Ring

Completing the cleaning
Wipe the inside of the nozzle and the threads at the ends of the spray-directing tube with moistened cotton-tipped swabs until the cotton comes away clean. Lubricate the nozzle and threads with a swab dipped in household oil. With the swab, oil the O-rings at each end of the tube *(above)* to prevent sticking and maintain sealing power. Reassemble the sprayer and fill the canister with water. Spray the water to flush the hose and pistol grip.

Clearing the outlet holes
Unscrew the spray-directing tube from the pistol grip, and remove the nozzle from the end of the tube. With a stiff wire, clear any residue from the outlet holes at the end of the tube *(above)*.

A NEW HANDLE FOR A LARGE TOOL

Removing a damaged handle

Secure the head of a large tool, such as the mattock shown at right, in a heavy vise. With a ¼-inch bit, drill four deep holes into the wood at the top of the handle as close as possible to the collar. Remove the tool from the vise, and tap the head with a small sledgehammer, driving it down toward the narrow part of the handle. If the head remains stuck, drill additional holes and tap harder.

Collar

Setting the new handle in place

Slip the mattock head onto the new handle. Drive the head into position with a small sledgehammer, forcing it over the wide section at the top of the handle (above); alternate the hammer blows from one side of the collar to the other to keep the head level. Set the mattock head in warm water overnight to swell the wood.

Making a tight fit

Let the wood dry. With a hammer, drive a ½-inch metal wedge—available at hardware stores—into the top of the handle across the grain of the wood (above). This should press the wood firmly against the collar. If the head of the tool is even slightly loose on the handle, drive additional wedges perpendicular to the first until the head is absolutely secure.

How to Be Your Own Landscape Designer

Like any major home-improvement project, landscaping calls for advance planning. Even a small lot is surprisingly flexible and warrants a systematic weighing of the design options that are available.

MAKING A MAP

Begin by creating a map of your property—the more detailed the better *(page 21)*. Include such factors as pleasing views and existing plantings. Note the locations of underground obstacles such as electric, water, and sewer lines, or dry wells, septic tanks, and cesspools; they will prevent or limit digging in certain areas.

PLANNING THE NEW YARD

Look at your lot as a whole and list all the important intended uses of your outdoor space—relaxation, storage, gardening, and so on. To some extent, the orientation of the house on the lot will define these areas: Traditionally, the house divides the lot into an approach area in the front yard; a private living area in the back; and an out-of-the-way service area, perhaps at the side of the house, for a set of trash cans or a toolshed. You may want to distinguish other areas—for games or work, say—and perhaps set them off with their own design elements.

ADDING DESIGN TOUCHES

Once you have outlined these areas, experiment on paper with the look of each one, keeping in mind the design principles explained at right and on the following two pages. At this stage, think of plantings in terms of their general visual attributes *(next page)* and such basic characteristics as whether they are evergreen or deciduous, flowering or nonflowering. Consider physical comfort in your planning. Hedges and fences can screen an area from the street or neighboring houses. A strategically placed tree will filter light or create shade and can lower the temperature on a patio by 15° to 20° F. A row of evergreen shrubs will shelter a walkway from winter winds. Choosing the specific plants that meet your criteria is the last step in the design process *(see appendix, pages 268-280)*.

VISUAL BUILDING BLOCKS

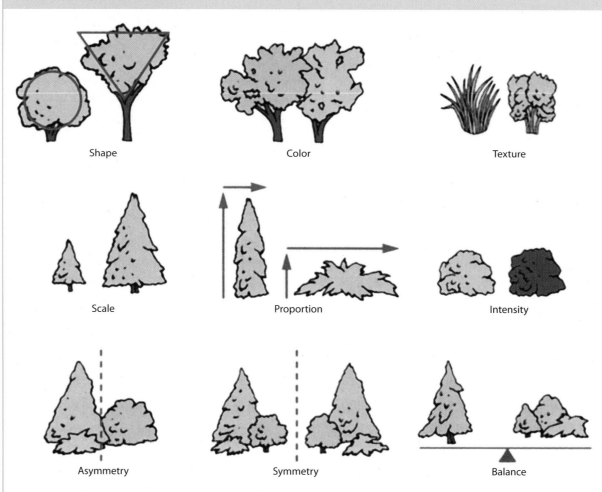

Shape

Color

Texture

Scale

Proportion

Intensity

Asymmetry

Symmetry

Balance

Each tree and shrub in a landscape has a number of visual attributes—shape, color, texture, scale (or size), proportions (the relationship between vertical and horizontal dimensions), and intensity of color. As you plan your design, picture how the visual qualities of the individual plantings will blend or contrast and how each tree or shrub might contribute to an overall feeling.

Design elements need to be considered not just individually but also in combinations. Terms such as *symmetry* or *balance* refer to their joint effects on the eye and mind.

A RANGE OF EFFECTS

Unity

Arrange the elements of your yard to create a unified picture—one in which the viewer's eye travels easily over the various elements, seeing them as parts of a whole. Above, two different borders of trees and shrubs both have a harmonious effect: In the top arrangement, the various sizes and shapes blend together casually; at bottom, the pattern of small and large plantings has a more formal unity.

Focal point

An element that attracts the eye is a focal point; it may be a door, bench, garden pool, arbor, specimen plant, or sculpture. Focal points are often at one end of a central axis, as at above left. The symmetrically planted flowers and shrubs accentuate the walk and draw the viewer's attention to the focal point—the front door. Another way to highlight an element is to place it in an area where it stands out; this can be off-center, as with the bench at above right. The shape of the garden leads the eye to the bench—the focal point for this view.

Balance

All landscape elements have a visual "weight." Good designs often balance their elements—large and small, light and dark, coarse and fine, dense and open—around a central point. In the asymmetrically balanced view at right, each side is different but the weights are similar: the group of shrubs balance the tall tree. A simpler route to balance would be through symmetry, designing a yard so that its two sides almost mirror each other.

Rhythm

The repeated use of similar patterns or shapes creates a visual rhythm by drawing the eye from one area to the next. Here, the outlined elements—the rectangular paving blocks, the planting beds, and the two trees along one side of the yard—provide a pleasant sense of movement.

Contrast

Alterations in materials, plants, textures, or lines can enliven a design. In this example, the stone path adds a new texture, and its curving shape breaks up the yard's straight lines. The vine-covered screen provides some variety because it contrasts with the rest of the fencing, and the different shapes of the trees also add interest.

Designing with geometry

Geometrical arrangements of plantings and paving can play
a major role in a landscape design. In the top example above,
rectangles and squares *(highlighted)* reflect and extend the straight
architectural lines of the house. Curves *(top, right)* do the opposite,
posing a strong and intriguing contrast to the house lines.
Triangles *(right)* direct the eye to a focal point—here, the expanse
of lawn in the center.

DRAFTING A NEW PLAN

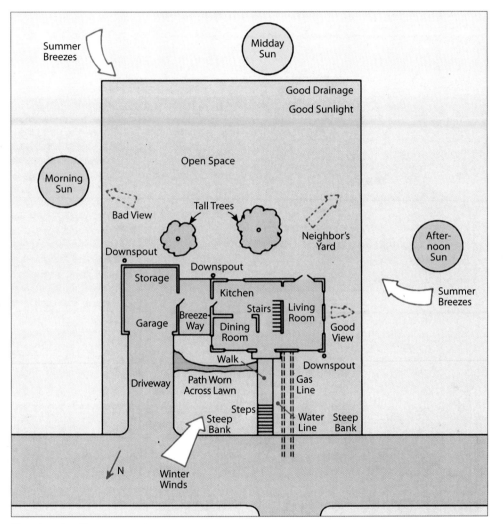

Mapping the site

On a sheet of graph paper, draw a map of your lot to scale. Then add a floor plan of the house's ground floor. Indicate good and bad views both from the windows of the house and from points within the yard; also note views into neighboring yards. Draw in existing trees, shrubs, flower beds, downspouts, and underground utilities; label steep banks, level areas, and spots with good drainage. Show the sun's morning, midday, and afternoon positions, as well as the direction of summer and winter winds.

Outlining use areas

Tape tracing paper over the lot map and outline some use areas for the major sections of your yard. In the plan at right, the lawn near the driveway is designated as the main approach area; a path has already been worn there. The plan calls for decorative plantings that will screen the street view from inside the house. The space behind the living room is defined as an outdoor living area. A well-drained, sunny corner of the yard is envisioned as a vegetable garden, with an adjacent utility area for tool storage.

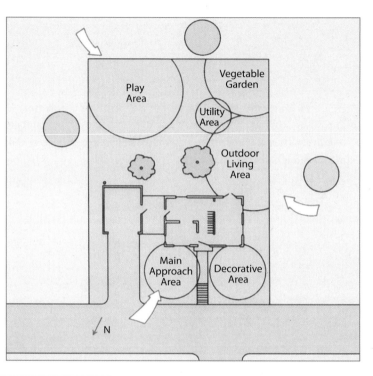

Experimenting with designs

Put a fresh sheet of tracing paper over your map, and experiment with designs for each of your circles on the previous map. Try to think of two or three different options for each area, remembering that you can remove things as well as add them. In the example at left, the old front steps are gone; instead, a paved walkway runs from the driveway to the front door. Decorative ground cover replaces hard-to-mow grass on the bank facing the street. In the back yard, the outdoor living area becomes a paved patio, and new shade trees and a high hedge block the afternoon sun and the neighbor's yard.

Moving Earth to Change the Lay of the Land

Many landscaping projects require that the contours of uneven ground be smoothed. Gardens, pools, patios, and playgrounds, for example, all need a level tract. Lawns, too, are more attractive and easier to maintain if they are relatively flat. Although some earth-moving jobs are extensive enough to warrant the hiring of an excavating company, a surprising amount of earth can be moved by hand, in short sessions of digging and hauling.

CLEARING AWAY OBSTACLES

Stones, stumps, logs, and other large debris must be removed before a site can be leveled. If a rock is too massive to be moved by the technique that is shown on page 25, either call in professional excavators or modify your landscape design to incorporate it—as the centerpiece of a rock garden, for example.

Don't try digging out a large tree stump by hand. Rather, rent a stump grinder; burn the stump with a special chemical solution sold in garden-supply centers; or cut the stump off just below ground level, cover it with dirt, and let it decompose naturally.

GRADING THE LAND

If a plot of land is perfectly flat, water will pool there during a rain. To ensure that water drains properly, grade the site so that it drops at least 1 inch vertically for every 4 horizontal feet. Make sure that the grade slopes away from the house.

If different parts of your yard slope in different directions, wait for a steady, heavy rain and observe the natural drainage patterns for an hour or so. Then establish the right grade for each part of the yard by the string-and-grid method described on pages 26-27.

FILLING IN LOW SPOTS

If you purchase earth to top off a grade, buy topsoil—a mix of earth and fertilizers from which stones, wood chips, and other debris have been removed—rather than fill, which often contains dense chunks of clay as well as rocks. A cubic yard of soil will cover 300 square feet of ground to a depth of 1 inch.

PROTECTING YOUR BACK

To avoid back injuries, lift heavy loads as much as possible with the muscles of your arms and legs. As a further precaution, wear a lower-back support—either a weightlifter's belt or a back-saver brace of the kind used by furniture movers.

TOOLS

- Spade
- Garden rake
- Metal rod or digging bar
- Sod cutter
- Line level
- Wooden stakes and string

MANAGING HEAVY LOADS WITHOUT STRAIN

The right way to wield a spade

Standing upright, set your foot atop the blade of the spade and force it deep into the earth. Place your hands in the positions that are shown in the second picture above, and push the top of the handle down, using the tool as a lever to dislodge the soil. Flex your knees and slide your lower hand down the handle for better leverage. Keeping your back as straight as possible, use your arms and legs to lift and pitch the soil *(third and fourth pictures)*.

A two-hand lift

Holding your torso erect, squat as close as possible to the load to be lifted *(far left)*. Keep the load close to your body and stand up slowly, using your legs—not your back—for lifting force *(middle left)*. To lessen strain on your back, hold the load close to your waist *(near left)*. When you turn, move your entire body, without twisting your torso.

A one-hand lift
Bending your knees slightly and keeping your back straight, lean forward from the waist to reach the load. Using your legs for lifting power and keeping your shoulders level, raise your body upright to lift the load. Extend your free arm for balance.

Clearing logs from a site
With a sturdy, rigid rod or digging bar, maneuver the log onto a roller—a smooth, cylindrical piece of wood or a section of iron pipe. Tie a rope around the forward end of the log. Pull the log slowly over the roller, slipping additional rollers under the forward end to keep the log supported. As each roller comes free at the back, move it to the front.

Moving a rock
With a rod or digging bar, lever a heavy stone—up to 100 pounds—onto a sheet of heavy canvas or burlap. Grasp the cloth firmly at both corners of one end, and use your arm and leg muscles to drag the rock from the site.

LEVELING AND GRADING A PLOT OF LAND

Skimming sod from the surface

With a sod cutter, remove the sod in strips from the area that will be leveled. If you intend to relay the sod on the plot after grading, gently roll up the strips, move them off the site, and unroll them again. Keep the sod well watered until you are ready for replanting.

Leveling ridges and depressions

Working when the soil is neither wet nor dry but slightly moist, transfer the dirt from obvious high spots in the plot to low spots. After you drop each spadeful, use the blade's end to break up compacted soil into chunks 1 inch across or less.

Setting a slope with stakes and strings

Drive stakes at the four corners of the plot. The stakes at the lowest corners (generally farthest from the house) should be tall enough to roughly match the level of the highest corners' stakes. Tie a string to one of the higher-corner stakes and stretch it along the side of the plot to the lower-corner stake opposite. As a helper checks a line level (*photograph*) hung from the string, raise or lower the string as necessary to level it. Mark the lower stake at the level of the string. Move the string down the stake to set the desired slope (*page 29*). Tie the string in place there. Repeat the procedure on the other side of the plot, then complete the boundary by tying leveled strings between the stakes at the top and the bottom of the plot.

Line Level

Laying out a grid

Drive stakes at 6-foot intervals just outside the strings that mark the boundaries of the plot. Create a grid over the area by tying a string between each opposite pair of stakes, setting the string at the level of the boundary strings. Make sure that the grid strings are taut.

Grading the surface

Working in one 6-foot square at a time, use a heavy rake to break up the soil to the consistency of coarse sand and spread it parallel to the plane of the string grid. Smooth the plot with the flat top side of the rake. Remove the stakes and strings.

Correcting Faulty Drainage

Professional landscapers define drainage as a two-stage process—the flow of water across the ground according to grade and the subsequent seepage of the water into the soil. In the first stage, rainwater can create problems in several ways: It can erode steep ground; it may flow to low areas and leave them soggy long after the rain has stopped; or it may pool around a house and perhaps find its way through the foundation.

A LOW-COST FIX FOR A WET BASEMENT

If a high water table or some other unseen problem is causing a wet basement, drainage professionals will have to be called in—but first check to see if the situation is simply a result of faulty surface drainage. In a 10-foot-wide zone around the house, the grade should drop at least 1 vertical inch for every horizontal foot.

Correct any insufficiency in the grade, and at the same time, use flexible plastic pipe to extend your gutter downspouts so that rainwater is channeled away from the house. Depending on the slope of your yard, the extension can end either in an underground dry well that traps and slowly disperses the water *(opposite)* or in a simple culvert that drains it away.

MANAGING HILL RUNOFF

To keep rainwater from collecting at the base of a gentle slope, divert the flow by constructing berms and swales—low earthen dams and shallow trenches *(page 30)*. For steeper slopes, the solution may be to terrace the land and build a retaining wall *(pages 31-35)*.

TOOLS	MATERIALS
■ Line level	■ Wooden stakes and string
■ Sod cutter	■ Flexible nonperforated drainpipe
■ Spade	■ Downspout adapter
■ Tamper	■ Splash block
■ Tape measure	■ Topsoil
	■ Gravel

DIVERTING WATER FROM THE FOUNDATION

String

Line Level

Tape
Measure

Checking the grade

Drive a stake next to the house and another one 10 feet away from the foundation. Tie a string between them and level it with a line level. Measure from the string to the ground at 1-foot intervals to calculate the grade. Move the stakes and repeat at other points along one side of the house. In any area where the grade drops less than 1 vertical inch for each horizontal foot, strip the sod *(page 26)* and remove any shrubs *(page 88)*. Dig a trench for the downspout extension; the trench should be 8 inches wide, a minimum of 10 feet long, and at least 6 inches deep at the downspout. It should also slope 1 inch per foot *(dashed lines, above)*.

Downspout
Adapter

Flexible
Drainpipe

Extending the downspout

Attach an adapter to the end of the downspout. Lay flexible nonperforated drainpipe in the trench and connect it to the adapter. The pipe must lie flat along the bottom of the trench without any dips or humps. Remove or add dirt under the pipe as necessary.

Making a dry well

At the end of the drainpipe trench, skim the sod from a 2½-foot-square area and set it aside. Then dig a hole about 3 feet deep. Pull the flexible drainpipe so that the lip protrudes a few inches over the hole. Fill in the trench with topsoil and tamp it down. Fill the hole with gravel to a point about 1 inch above the top of the pipe. Add topsoil and replace the sod (above). If the trench ends on a slope, lead the pipe out of the hill and onto a splash block (inset). The block will prevent erosion at the outlet point.

Correcting the grade

When the drainpipe extension is complete, correct any improper grade around the house. If you are piling dirt higher against the foundation, first treat the masonry with a waterproofing sealant. The soil level must remain at least 6 inches below wooden siding in order to keep termites out. Use a tamper to pack the soil firmly.

CONTROLLING RUNOFF ON A GENTLE SLOPE

Creating berms and swales

Dig a trench, or swale, about 3 inches deep and at least twice that wide across the slope above the area you wish to protect. Create a berm by piling the leftover soil into a gently rounded mound below the swale, then tamp it down. Lay sod (page 68) on the berm and the swale or plant a ground cover (page 69).

A Timber Retaining Wall

Terracing slopes with timber retaining walls not only solves erosion problems but can also add to the visual appeal of yards and gardens. Because earth and water create tremendous pressures behind a retaining wall, you must make the structure strong and provide for adequate drainage.

The design described on the following pages meets these requirements; moreover, it is easy to build, presents a trim face unmarked by nails or fasteners, and in most localities requires no building permit. This design, however, is not suitable for walls that are more than 3 feet high; they call for both a permit and the services of a structural engineer. If you have a long, steep slope, consider terracing it at intervals with two or more 3-foot walls.

CHOOSING THE MATERIAL

Wooden retaining walls can be made of any timbers that have been treated to resist rot and termites. Railroad ties were once the material of choice, but they have fallen out of favor because the wood is treated with the preservative creosote, which is poisonous to many plants.

Pressure-treated 6-by 6-inch timbers of poplar or pine, either rough- or smooth-sawed, are excellent alternatives. They are treated with environmentally safe preservatives and come in convenient 8-foot lengths, which can be cut as needed with a chain saw *(box, next page)*.

WHERE TO PLACE THE WALL

If you build the wall near the bottom of the slope, you will need to add fill dirt behind it. Alternatively, you can excavate higher up, erect the wall against the slope's face, and cart away the leftover dirt. The first option increases your level yard space above the wall; the second, below it.

TOOLS

- Line level
- Shovel
- Hand- or gas-powered tamper
- Carpenter's level
- Chain saw
- Heavy-duty drill with a ⅜-inch bit 18 inches long
- Long-handled sledgehammer

MATERIALS

- Wooden stakes and string
- Gravel
- 6-by-6 pressure-treated timbers of poplar or pine
- Galvanized screen and nails
- ⅜-inch reinforcing steel bars 42 inches long
- ⅜-inch galvanized spikes 12 inches long
- 4-inch perforated drain tile

CAUTION

Before excavating, establish the locations of possible underground obstacles such as dry wells, septic tanks, and cesspools, and electric, water, and sewer lines.

USING A CHAIN SAW SAFELY

Be sure the cutting teeth are sharp and the chain is at the proper tension: You should never be able to pull it more than ⅛ inch away from the bar. Steady the timbers on solid supports for sawing, and chalk cutting lines on the timbers as guides. Wear goggles to protect your eyes from flying woodchips. Brace the saw firmly on the ground before starting it, and hold the saw with both hands when cutting. Because pressure-treated lumber contains pesticides, wear a dust mask when sawing it and wash your hands thoroughly afterward.

Deadman

Drain Tile

Gravel

1" Drainage Gap

42" Spike

Anatomy of a retaining wall

The bottom course in this 3-foot retaining wall is set in a trench and anchored by 42-inch-long bars of ⅜-inch reinforcing steel, or rebar. Successive courses are secured with 12-inch galvanized spikes. Several features help the wall withstand the pressure of earth and water behind it. Each course is staggered ½ inch toward the slope. Reinforcing timbers—deadmen run 8 feet back into the hillside and rest on 1-foot-long timber crossplates anchored with 42-inch spikes. Sidewalls are built up on the corner deadmen and connected to the wall by interlocked corners. Four-inch perforated drain tile buried in gravel and 1-inch gaps between adjacent timbers in the second course provide escape routes for the water behind the wall.

PREPARING THE SITE

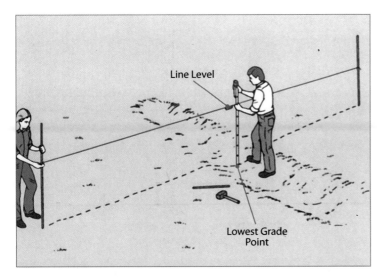

Line Level

Lowest Grade
Point

Marking the wall trench
Drive 5-foot stakes at the points you have chosen for the corners of the wall. Tie a line between the stakes, and level it with a line level. Measure to find the point where the line is farthest from ground level *(left)*. This is the lowest grade point; mark it with a stake. Drop a plumb line every 4 feet along the line, and drive stakes at these points to mark the outer edge of the wall. Transfer the line from the 5-foot stakes to the lower stakes.

Digging the trench
Starting at the lowest grade point and working out to the corner stakes, dig a level-bottomed trench that is 1 foot deep at the lowest grade point and 1 foot wide along its full length. Spread a 6-inch layer of gravel in the trench and tamp it down. Check the base of the trench with a carpenter's level. Remove the stakes. Lay the timbers for the first course in the trench. Their tops should be even with ground level at the lowest grade point. To lay out deadman trenches, start at one corner and stretch an 8-foot line at right angles to the wall; drive a stake at the end of the line. Repeat at the other corner and at 6-foot intervals in between.

BUILDING THE WALL

Securing the first two courses

At the center of each timber and 6 inches from each end, drill vertical holes completely through, using the ⅜-inch bit. Then drive 42-inch spikes through the holes and into the ground with a sledgehammer *(right)*. Lay the second course so that the joints between timbers do not coincide with those of the first. Set the second course ½ inch closer to the hillside, and leave 1-inch gaps between timbers to serve as drainage holes. Drill three holes through each timber, and drive 12-inch spikes through the holes to pin the first two courses together.

Bracing the wall

For the deadmen, dig trenches—their bottoms level with the top of the second course—back to the stakes. Across the ends of the deadman trenches, dig crossplate trenches 3 feet long and 6 inches deeper than the deadman trenches at that point. Lay the crossplates in place, then set the deadmen on top of them so their other ends rest on the second course, ½ inch back from the front face. Drill pilot holes and drive 42-inch spikes through the deadmen and the cross-plates and into the ground. Drive 12-inch spikes through the deadmen into the second course. For the third course of the wall, cut timbers to fit between the deadmen—making sure that the joints don't align with those of the second course—and secure them with spikes.

Laying a drainage run

On the back of the wall, nail pieces of galvanized screen over the drainage gaps in the second course of timbers. Shovel a bed of gravel behind the wall, leaving enough space to run a length of 4-inch perforated drain tile along the top of the bed and under the deadmen *(above)*. Then add another 6 inches of gravel.

Interlocking the corners

After completing the fourth course of timbers, lay a sidewall timber at each end of the wall and secure it to the corner deadman with 12-inch spikes. Lay another sidewall timber atop the first so that its end is set back ½ inch from the face of the fourth course. Secure it with spikes. Fit the timbers for the fifth course between the sidewall timbers, fastening them with spikes. Continue laying the front and sidewall courses in this manner, making sure to offset the timber joints between courses and stagger each course ½ inch closer to the hillside. Then drill horizontal holes through the corner deadmen and those sidewall courses that extend to the front of the wall, and drive 12-inch spikes to secure the corners *(left)*. Spread a 4-inch layer of soil behind the wall and tamp it with a hand- or gas-powered tamper. Spread and tamp additional 4-inch layers until the fill is level with the top of the wall.

Preparing Soil for Planting

All soils are composed primarily of mineral particles, ranging in size from fine, dense clay to medium-size silt to coarse, loose sand. The proportions of these ingredients—along with decayed vegetable and animal matter, known as humus—determine the texture and quality of the soil. Soil that has too much clay in it retains water almost indefinitely, causing problems with drainage. Sandy soil dries too quickly and allows nutrients to leach out.

The best garden soil is called loam and is a balance of clay, silt, and sand, with plenty of humus to help hold the mineral particles together and aid in the retention of moisture. Crumbly in texture, loam has plentiful spaces to let both air and excess water pass through, while nutrients are retained. Humus keeps the soil fertile and makes the soil easy to work.

Proper texture is only one requirement of good garden soil. In addition, the soil must contain nutrients necessary for plant growth, and it should be neither too acidic nor too alkaline—conditions that impair the ability of roots to extract the nutrients from the soil.

A SOIL DIAGNOSIS

With a few simple tests, you can evaluate your soil's texture and chemical composition. The water test shown at right can gauge the need for texture-improving organic amendments. Peat moss and dehydrated manure are two widely used amendments, but the best of all is compost; it adds nutrients as well as improving soil structure—and you can make it in your backyard *(page 41)*.

For chemical tests, use an inexpensive soil-test kit, available at garden centers. Most of these kits contain an array of test vials and chemicals, along with charts for interpreting the results. There are tests for nitrogen, phosphorus, potassium, and—most important of all—the degree of acidity or alkalinity, known as pH.

GETTING THE CORRECT pH

The scale that measures pH runs from 0 to 14. Neutral soil has a pH of 7. Above 7, soil is increasingly alkaline; below 7, it is increasingly acid. Most plants grow best in slightly acid soil, with a pH level between 6 and 7; consult the appendix for plant preferences.

To reduce acidity, add dolomitic limestone, which includes magnesium, an essential nutrient. In light, sandy soil, 4 pounds per every 100 square feet will raise the pH by .5; add 20 percent to this formula for loamy soil and 30 percent in heavy, clayey soil.

Excess alkalinity is corrected by adding sulfur—either pure ground sulfur, iron sulfate, or aluminum sulfate. Pure sulfur acts more slowly than the others but lasts longer; iron sulfate puts iron in the soil, producing lush, dark foliage; aluminum sulfate must be used cautiously because too much aluminum can be harmful to plants.

To reduce the alkalinity in 100 square feet of sandy soil by a pH interval of .5 to 1, use 3 to 5 pounds of iron or aluminum sulfate, or ½ to ¾ pound of ground sulfur; use 1½ times as much in loamy soil, 4 times as much in clayey soil.

WHEN AND HOW TO ENRICH THE SOIL

Add amendments to your soil 4 to 6 months before planting, to give them time to become thoroughly incorporated. Mix in organic amendments by tilling the soil *(page 40)*. Broadcast dolomitic limestone or sulfur on the surface, then rake it into the top few inches.

For a small area, you can do the tilling with a spade and spading fork *(page 40)*. To till a large area quickly and easily, rent a power tiller. A model that has the tines set behind the engine is more stable and generally preferable for a beginner; a model with tines mounted on the front is more maneuverable in tight places.

Do not till soggy soil; it will break up into large, heavy clods that can dry as hard as rocks. A good time for tilling is generally 3 days after a rain, when the soil is neither too wet nor so dry that the job creates annoying dust.

TOOLS	MATERIALS
■ Spade	■ Manure
■ Bucket	■ Peat moss
■ Trowel	■ Compost
■ Ruler	■ Dolomitic limestone
■ Test kit	■ Sulfur
■ Tarp	
■ Spading fork	
■ Power tiller	

ANALYZING TEXTURE AND CHEMISTRY

Gathering samples
At several different spots within the area you intend to plant, dig holes about 6 inches wide and 6 to 9 inches deep. Slice a thin wedge of soil from the wall of each hole *(right)*. Wearing gloves so that your hands do not affect soil chemistry, remove sod and any small stones or roots from the samples, then mix them all together in a plastic bucket with the spade or a trowel.

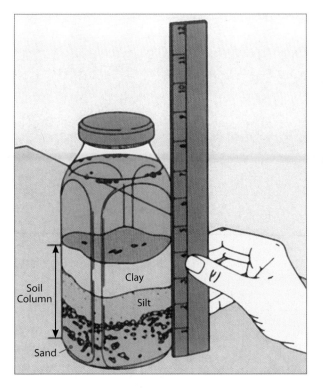

A water test for texture

Fill a quart bottle half full with water and add soil until the bottle is nearly full. Cap the bottle, shake it well, then wait for the soil particles to settle in layers—from 3 hours to a day. Measure the thickness of each layer—clay on top, silt in the middle, and sand on the bottom—and divide it by the total height of the soil column to get each component's percentage. When you adjust your soil's texture with organic amendments *(page 41)*, add about 2 or 3 inches of peat moss, manure, or compost if the soil is less than 25 percent silt or more than 25 percent clay. For soil that is more than 30 percent sand, add twice as much.

Testing the pH level

Fill the pH test chamber of a soil test kit to the correct mark with soil and add the amount of chemical called for in the kit's directions. Using an eyedropper, fill the chamber with water up to the indicated line *(right)*. Cap the chamber and shake it to mix the soil and the liquid thoroughly. After the soil particles settle, compare the color of the remaining solution with the kit's color chart. The closest match of colors indicates your soil's pH level.

MODIFYING SOIL TO IMPROVE IT

Soil Amendments

Turning the soil by hand

With the point of a spade, outline the area to be worked and divide it into sections 2 feet wide. Dig out the soil from an end section to the full depth of the spade (6 to 9 inches), depositing the soil on a plastic sheet or tarp *(above, left)*. Then fill this trench with soil from the adjacent section *(above, right)*. Spread the desired organic soil amendments *(page 37)* on the first section and work them in with a spading fork. Transfer the top 9 inches of soil from the third section to fill up the second, and add amendments. Continue in this way until you reach the last section. Fill the last trench with the original soil from the first section.

Operating a power tiller

Put the tiller in neutral, position it at one corner of the planting area, and set the tines to the correct depth—from 3 inches for heavy, clayey soil to 8 inches for sandy soil. Start the engine, shift into forward, and guide the machine along one side of the bed. Make a broad turn at the far end, and work back in the opposite direction, creating a U-shaped area of tilled soil. Continue back and forth until you reach the end, then reverse directions and repeat the pattern in the untilled strips *(inset)*. If your soil is very heavy, set the tines at 6 inches and till again. Spread the desired amount of organic soil amendments *(page 37)* on top of the soil. Set the tines at maximum depth and till in a direction perpendicular to the first set of lines to work in the amendments. If the tiller bucks excessively, go more slowly and raise the tines slightly.

THE COMPOST PILE: FREE FERTILIZER FROM THROWAWAYS

Making compost is somewhat like setting up a fertilizer factory in your own backyard. If organic matter is simply heaped in a pile, the composting process can take up to a year. But if you place the materials in bins that distribute heat and moisture evenly, you will have usable compost in just 3 or 4 weeks. The most efficient composting system uses three bins: one for fresh organic material, one for half-decomposed matter, and one for the finished product. You can buy bins—plastic barrels, for example—or you can make them.

One easy-to-build arrangement is shown below. These bins are 4 feet high and 3 feet square. No floor is necessary. The vertical posts, set into the ground for stability, are 2-by-4s. Grooves cut into the front posts with a router or circular saw allow 1-by-6 slats to slide in and out for easy turning of the compost.

Air circulation around the pile is very important. Here, the front slats are held apart by screws that are driven into one side of the boards. The sides and backs of the bins are heavy-gauge wire screening, held in place by 1-by-6 boards nailed to the top and bottom of the posts.

THE INGREDIENTS

To start a compost pile, you need equal proportions of so-called "browns" (shredded sticks, sawdust, and leaves) and "greens" (grass and hedge clippings, garden refuse, and vegetable scraps). Other organic materials, such as wood ashes, fruit peels, crushed eggshells, and coffee grounds, are also helpful. Do not include diseased plants, invasive weeds, pet droppings, or cooked scraps, which will attract vermin.

Place 6 inches of coarse brown material on the bottom. Then add an inch of commercial manure to provide food for the microorganisms, followed by 6 inches of green material, another inch of manure, and an inch of soil. Water until damp, then keep stacking layers in the same sequence and proportions until the bin is full.

COOKING THE PILE

Leave the pile alone for a few days, then start turning it with a spading fork several times a week to speed decomposition. After a couple of weeks, shift part of the pile to the next bin, and add fresh kitchen and yard waste to the first; layering does not matter now.

Water both bins occasionally to keep the piles moist. In another 2 weeks, the compost in the second bin should be dark and crumbly; store it in the third bin until ready for use.

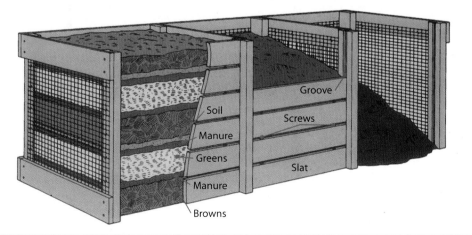

Groove

Soil

Manure

Screws

Greens

Slat

Manure

Browns

CHAPTER 2

Growing a Blanket of Green

For many, landscaping begins and ends with the lawn—and for good reason. There is no escaping a continuous regimen of lawn upkeep throughout the growing season. A less burdensome alternative is to plant a low-maintenance ground cover such as ivy or periwinkle. Whatever your choice, this chapter holds the keys to a verdant backdrop for your house that will retain its beauty year after year.

Rolls of sod will make your lawn instantly green, but require daily care until they root properly.

Neat edges add to the well-manicured appearance of these lawns.

Lush stretches of green lawn can serve as the focal point of a landscaping design or as a canvas to set off colorful floral displays and seasonal shrubs or trees.

Getting your lawn this level and well-drained may take some work, but the results speak for themselves.

Maintaining a Healthy Lawn

Expanses of weed-free, perfectly groomed grass do not occur naturally; they require careful attention and consistent care. Along with the routine demands of mowing and watering, other periodic tasks such as fertilizing, aerating, and dethatching are also necessary to keep the grass green and healthy.

CUTTING THE GRASS

There are a wide variety of mowers available; choose the one that best suits your needs. Sharpen the blade yearly *(page 11)* and keep the lawn free of debris that might dull the blade or be thrown out of the mower's chute. Before starting the engine, adjust the cutting height *(page 50)*. Recommended mowing heights for the most common lawn grasses are given in the appendix.

Lawn clippings can be bagged, but short clippings left on the lawn decompose to a natural fertilizer. Modern mulching mowers, which have a special blade and a fully enclosed deck, chop clippings fine to speed decomposition; you may be able to convert an older mower to work like a mulcher.

For a finished appearance, crop around posts and other hard-to-reach areas with a power trimmer, and use an edger to cut a small, narrow trench along flower beds and sidewalks *(page 51)*.

PROVIDING WATER AND FOOD

In summer, when high heat and lower rainfall slow the growth of grass, you will mow your lawn less often but water it more. A thorough watering—perhaps once a week—is preferable to frequent light waterings, which can inhibit the growth of deep roots. Control the amount of water the lawn receives by setting your sprinkler for the correct intensity and area.

Grass does not, of course, live by water alone. To replace soil nutrients, fertilizers must be added. The timing depends on the type of grass, as indicated in the grasses chart. Always sweep excess fertilizer from sidewalks and driveways onto the lawn to prevent runoff into storm drains.

CONTROLLING WEEDS

Even in the best-kept lawn, a few weeds are inevitable and must be dug up or destroyed with a selective herbicide that kills weeds without harming grass. Some weed-killers wither parts of the plant they touch. Others are systemic: they are absorbed into the plant, destroying even the roots. Weed-killers can be applied directly to isolated weeds or they can be sprayed over an entire area that is badly infested *(pages 57-58)*.

Most large garden centers carry water-soluble, environmentally safe dyes that when mixed with herbicides in the sprayer help ensure even coverage. Rain or watering soon washes the dye away.

STIMULATING GROWTH

Despite careful watering and fertilizing, a lawn may still deteriorate if thatch—a matted layer of dead grass—becomes too thick, strangling new growth. Strip it off with a thatch rake or a power dethatcher *(page 60)*; both devices cut slits through the tightly woven barrier so it can easily be raked away.

The soil in heavily used backyards or play areas can become so compacted that grass roots cannot penetrate it. An aerator *(page 61)*, which extracts small plugs of earth to loosen compacted soil, may be needed as often as every 2 years. Periodic aeration also helps prevent thatch buildup.

Compost is an excellent soil amendment, or additive, when raked into the holes left by the aerator. Contact your local extension service to see if composted municipal sludge is available in your area.

TOOLS	MATERIALS
■ Tape measure	■ Lawn fertilizer
■ Screwdriver	■ Grass seed
■ Weeding fork	■ Weed-killer
■ Spading fork	■ Stakes
■ Garden rake	■ String
■ Hoe	■ Peat moss
■ Garden trowel	■ Composted municipal sludge
■ Thatch rake or power dethatcher	■ Straw or wood fiber mulch
■ Grass rake	■ Chain-link fencing
■ Aerating fork or power aerator	

CAUTION

Before repairing or adjusting power lawn-care equipment, always unplug an electrically powered machine, or if it has a gasoline engine, disconnect the spark plug wire.

SAFETY TIP

When using lawn-care machinery wear sturdy leather shoes (preferably steel-tipped), long pants, goggles, and gloves. Also protect your ears when operating loud gasoline-powered machines. Wear gloves when using hand tools to dig or rake.

EQUIPMENT FOR MOWING AND TRIMMING

A reel mower
The scissoring action of reel blades against a fixed metal bed knife makes a smooth cut, particularly on thin grasses such as bluegrass. Reel mowers are less effective in trimming denser grasses such as zoysia. The blades need frequent sharpening and are easily damaged by twigs or pebbles. In addition to the manual mower shown here, there are also self-propelled power models. Both types are best suited for small, level lawns.

Reel Blades

Roller   Bed Knife

The versatile rotary mower
A walk-behind mower like the one shown at right cuts a clean swath through any type of grass and allows you to bag your clippings, discharge them, or mulch them. Similar features are available in riding mowers, which may be worth their extra cost for lawns larger than ½ acre. Essential to mulching is a mulching blade *(photograph)*, which is specially curved to lift and slice the grass repeatedly over a long cutting edge.

Mulching Blade

A power trimmer

Available in gas, plug-in, or battery-powered models, this tool is handy for cropping grass around posts and other obstacles to lawn mowers. A rotating nylon cord lops off grass with a whipping action. Cord frayed through use is replaced from a reel in the cutting head, which when tapped on the ground releases a length of fresh cord. A cutter on the safety guard trims the cord to the correct length.

Cutter

Cutting Head

Nylon Cord

A power edger

Trimming along a walk or driveway with an electric or gasoline-powered edger gives a neat, finished look to a lawn. A metal edge guide prevents the machine from wandering while the spinning blade digs a shallow trench along the edge.

Blade

Guide

MANICURING YOUR LAWN

Setting the mower blade height

Roll the lawn mower onto a driveway or sidewalk and detach the spark plug wire. (Unplug electric models.) Reach into the discharge chute and rotate the blade so that one end is toward you, then measure the distance from the blade to the ground. Move the height-adjustment levers *(right)*, raising or lowering the deck to achieve the desired blade height—usually between 1 and 2 inches.

Deck

Spark Plug Wire

Height-Adjustment Levers

Mowing on level lawns and slopes

On a level lawn, the choice of mowing pattern is up to you. But whether you cut in parallel strips up and down the lawn or in an elongated spiral as shown at left, remember that mowing affects the direction in which grass grows and leans. To prevent stripes in the lawn, change the direction of the pattern each time you mow. To mow safely on a hillside *(inset)*, begin at the top of the slope, and guide a walk-behind power mower across it in parallel lines. With a riding mower, drive up and down the slope for the best stability.

Trimming around obstacles

Hold the power trimmer's cutting head parallel to the ground, an inch or so above the soil, and swing the cutter back and forth in smooth passes, working toward the obstacle.

Cutting a clean edge

For short lengths of edging along sidewalks, driveways, and flower beds, a manual rotary edger may be sufficient, but for bigger jobs, use a power edger *(right)*. If the blade of your edger is adjustable, set it to the desired depth. Then position the edger so the wheels are on the hard surface. Turn on the machine and walk at a steady pace, pressing the guide against the edge of the pavement or border.

Guide

CHOOSING THE RIGHT SPRINKLER

An oscillating sprinkler
Driven by water pressure from a garden hose, an oscillating sprinkler provides an even dousing of a rectangular area of grass. The perforated, curved crosspiece swings back and forth through all or part of an arc; controls at the base of the crosspiece set the sprinkler to water all of the lawn, the center alone, or either half *(shaded areas, left)*.

TESTING YOUR SPRINKLER COVERAGE

To check the quantity and distribution of water from your sprinkler, set several shallow containers, such as empty tuna cans, throughout the area to be watered, then run the sprinkler for an hour at the same time of day you water the lawn. You should expect to collect 1 inch of water in an hour, and the amounts of water in each can should be almost equal.

Test for water penetration by pushing a screwdriver tip into the lawn 24 hours after watering it. If you encounter resistance before the tip reaches a depth of 6 inches, water the lawn longer.

A turret sprinkler

Multiple sprinkler heads on the turret spray rectangular patterns of different lengths and widths. Compared with an oscillator, a turret sprinkler provides a dousing that is quick, heavy, and somewhat uneven.

Sprinkler Heads

Turret

A pulsating sprinkler

The head of this sprinkler waters grass in a circular pattern that can be adjusted from a narrow wedge to a full circle. The sprinkler head is constantly in motion to prevent water from pooling, and the stream can be varied from a fine spray for small areas to a heavy, longer-range jet.

A traveling sprinkler

This self-propelled sprinkler is ideal for long, narrow lawns. Using its own hose as a track, it creeps along the route even uphill, while the spinning nozzles soak the grass. The traveling sprinkler shown here drags its hose behind it; other models reel in the slack hose as they move across the grass.

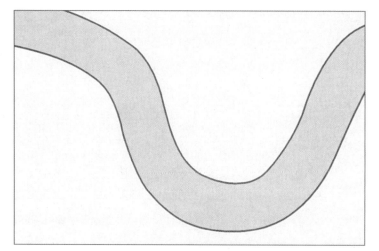

A sprinkler hose

Tiny holes along the top of the hose provide a fine, soaking mist. The flexible hose is especially suited for very narrow areas. It can also be laid to match an irregular plot's contours *(left)*.

APPLYING FERTILIZER

Release Lever

End Rows

Spreader Gauge

Calculating the quantity

To determine how much fertilizer you need for your lawn, divide the grassy area into rough geometric shapes such as rectangles, circles, and triangles *(above)*. Calculate the area of each section, then add those figures together. Small areas outside the lawn that happen to be included in this estimate tend to compensate for grassy patches that are left out.

Using a trough spreader

Set the spreader gauge according to the instructions on the fertilizer package. At a corner of the lawn, open the trough with the release lever and immediately start walking at an even, moderate pace along one side of the lawn. Close the trough when you reach the far end to avoid burning the grass with excess fertilizer. Turn the spreader around and position it so that the next row touches but does not overlap the first. Open the trough and run the second row, then make two similar rows at the opposite end of the lawn *(inset)*. Fill in the remaining area by running rows perpendicular to the end rows, being careful not to overlap the fertilizer at any point.

WHAT TO LOOK FOR IN A FERTILIZER

Lawn fertilizers come in liquid, pellet, and granular form, with labels that rate the nitrogen, phosphorus, and potassium content according to a three-number code. For example, one common rating, 10-6-4, indicates that 10 percent of the fertilizer bulk is nitrogen, 6 percent phosphorus, and 4 percent potassium. Make a soil test *(page 39)* annually to check for deficiency in any of these three minerals. If the soil is found wanting in one of them, use fertilizer with a higher proportion of the mineral in short supply.

Liquid fertilizer is easy to apply, but the nutrients leach through the soil quickly, necessitating frequent reapplication. Although time-release pellets last 6 months or more, they are costly and slow acting. The more common choice is dry granular fertilizer because it is quick, reliable, and relatively inexpensive.

Using a broadcast spreader

Calibrate the spreader according to the fertilizer directions, then, beginning at a corner of the lawn, push the spreader at a steady pace that scatters fertilizer 3 or 4 feet to each side. Work up and down the lawn in wide parallel sweeps. To ensure full coverage near the edges of the path where the fertilizer falls less densely, overlap the rows by about 1 foot. Approach corners and boundaries close enough to give them full coverage. Repeat the pattern at a right angle to the original rows *(inset)*.

> ### CAUTION
>
> Fertilizers, weed-killers, and other chemicals can be harmful if they come in contact with the skin. Read the labels carefully and follow their recommendations. In addition to long pants and a long-sleeved shirt, it is advisable to wear rubber gloves and eye protection. A dust mask traps particles of dry fertilizers.

SPOT TREATMENTS FOR ISOLATED WEEDS

A weeding fork

If the soil around the weed is hard, soften it by watering over a period of days. Grasp the runners or leaves in one hand; with the other, push a weeding fork 3 or 4 inches into the earth alongside the main root. For an unusually stubborn weed, dig the fork all the way around it, trying not to tear the leaves or break the roots. Lever the fork in the surrounding soil to work the roots free, then pull up lightly on the bunched leaves to remove the weed with its roots intact. Sprinkle a few grass seeds in the hole that has been left by the weed.

A trigger sprayer

Hold the bottle of weed-killer above the weed, and spray directly onto the center of the plant, coating the leaves and main stem. Allow 2 to 4 weeks for the weed to shrivel and die, then remove it.

WEED-KILLER CHECKLIST

✔ Unless an area is badly infested with weeds, spot-treat individual plants rather than treating the entire area.

✔ Spray weed-killers on calm, still days.

✔ To expose the greatest surface area of the weed to the weed-killer, postpone mowing until at least 2 days after applying the chemical.

✔ Keep clippings from grass that has been treated with weed-killers out of mulch or compost used in gardens or around shrubs. Residual chemicals may harm other plants.

✔ Observe the cautions noted on page 56.

SPRAYING WEED-KILLER OVER A LARGE AREA

Using a pressurized sprayer

Along one end of the weed-infested area, mark off a 3-yard strip with a pair of staked parallel strings. Build up pressure in the sprayer with a few strokes of the hand pump, then spray the area between the strings, holding the wand about 12 inches above the lawn and moving it quickly and steadily for a light, even coverage. Move one of the strings to mark off an adjoining strip, and treat this area in the same way. Continue spraying strips until you have covered the entire area.

Using a garden-hose sprayer

Read the weed-killer's label to see how many square feet one jarful will cover, mark off that area with string and stakes, then run a string down the middle to divide it in half. Fill the sprayer jar with the weed-killer-and-water mixture specified in the label instructions; then screw the sprayer nozzle onto a garden hose and attach the jar to the nozzle. Turn on the hose and start the flow of weed-killer by covering the air-siphon hole with your thumb or by depressing the trigger, depending on your model. Spray half the weed-killer evenly on one side of the string, then apply the remainder on the other side.

RESEEDING A BARE PATCH

Preparing the soil
Turn the soil in the plot with a spading fork, digging 5 or 6 inches deep. Remove 3 inches of soil and work the remainder to break up clods. Dust the area lightly with lawn fertilizer and add a 3-inch layer of composted municipal sludge or peat moss, then use the spading fork to mix it thoroughly with the underlying soil. Make the soil even with the surrounding earth by tamping it down with your foot. If necessary, adjust the soil level, either by removing mix or by adding and tamping down more made from the 3 inches of soil removed from the area. Smooth the surface of the soil with the back of a garden rake.

Reseeding the patch
With your thumb and forefinger, sprinkle grass seeds ⅛ inch apart over the patch *(right)*. Work the seeds into the top ⅛ inch of soil mix with a garden rake, then tamp the soil lightly with the back of a hoe. Cover the patch with a thin layer of straw—half the soil should show through—to protect the seeds from birds and wind, and lightly mist the area with a garden hose.

CUTTING THROUGH LAYERS OF THATCH

Checking for thatch buildup

Pierce the lawn with a garden trowel and pull the slit open to expose the layers of grass, roots, and soil *(right)*. Check for a matted layer of densely intertwined roots and dead grass between the green blades and the soil *(inset)*. If this layer is thicker than ½ inch, dethatch the lawn.

Thatch

Soil

Thatch

Clutch

Blade-Height Lever

Adjustment Knob

Dethatching the lawn

For a small plot, work in rows about 2 feet wide with a thatch rake *(above, left)*. Hold the rake at a 30-degree angle and press the teeth through the thatch. Pull the rake through the grass to dislodge the thatch. For large areas, rent a self-propelled power dethatcher *(above, right)*. At the center of the lawn, pull the height lever to lower the blades into the thatch, then turn the adjustment knob until the blades barely penetrate the soil. Engage the clutch, then run the machine over the lawn. Follow the pattern used for mowing *(page 50)*, but do not overlap the rows. Remove the thatch with a flexible grass rake.

BREAKING UP COMPACTED SOIL

Clutch Lever

Corer Drum

Aerating the lawn

Mow the lawn and saturate the ground with a sprinkler a day in advance of when you plan to aerate. For a small lawn, thrust an aerating fork with three or four tines *(above, left)* into the ground at 6-inch intervals; try to penetrate to a depth of at least 3 inches. If the soil is too compacted, make a shallower pass, resoak the lawn, and try again. Work along one boundary, and then back and forth parallel to this line, leaving the extracted cores scattered on the ground. For large areas, rent a power aerator *(above, right)*. Beginning at the center of the lawn, start the aerator's engine and warm it up with the clutch disengaged. Engage the clutch to start the corer drum, and guide the aerator in the pattern that is used for mowing, but do not overlap rows. In particularly hard soil you may need to increase penetration either by adding water to the corer drum or by attaching weights, if they were provided, or both.

Crumbling the cores

For a small area, use the back of a garden rake to break up the cores *(left)* and spread a ½-inch layer of composted municipal sludge or other soil amendment over the area, filling the core holes. Water the lawn thoroughly. For larger lawns, drag a section of chain-link fencing across the lawn—either by hand or attached to a lawn tractor—to break up the cores.

Growing a New Lawn

Whether establishing a new lawn on an empty lot or replacing an old one that is terminally choked with weeds, you must start the job from scratch. Although not complicated, the process requires careful planning and hard work.

CHOOSING THE RIGHT GRASS

The type of grass you plant depends largely upon the local climate. Cool-season grasses, so called because they grow rapidly in the cool temperatures of spring and autumn while languishing in the warm months of a relatively short summer, do well in northern climates. Warm-season grasses, which are more suited to southern climates, flourish in the heat of a long summer and are dormant in cool months. In regions with wide variations of temperature, a mixture of grasses gives the best results.

Check the grass chart on pages 265 and 266 for other characteristics such as color, texture, and drought tolerance that you should consider when choosing a grass.

SELECTING A PLANTING METHOD

How you plant your new lawn depends primarily upon the kind of grass you plan to grow and on how quickly you want the lawn to be established.

Seeding *(page 64)* is the least expensive way to start a lawn and offers the greatest choice of grasses. It is also the slowest because the plants must sprout before they can begin to spread and fill in the lawn. Planting alternatives for warm-season grasses and for sterile hybrids, which produce no seeds, are sprigging *(page 65)* and plugging *(page 66)*. Sprigs and plugs generally fill in faster than a seeded lawn and, in the meantime, are less fragile. In both cases, the sparsely planted mature plants send out new shoots that fill the gaps in between.

The quickest—and most expensive—way to a new lawn is sodding, in which long strips of fully developed turf are set on bare ground *(page 68)*. Lay sod within 36 hours of its harvest, and have your plot ready before the delivery date. For large lawns, consider having the sod delivered in installments so it does not dry out before planting.

PREPARING THE SITE

No matter which planting method you choose, you must carefully prepare the planting bed *(opposite)*. Before replacing a weed-infested lawn, apply a systemic herbicide formulated to kill all plant life. Follow the manufacturer's instructions, allowing the chemical to dissipate before replanting. Use a sod cutter to remove the old turf, and prepare and smooth the bed *(pages 63-64)*.

TOOLS	MATERIALS
■ Sod cutter	■ Straw
■ Tiller	■ 3½-inch nails
■ Garden rake	■ 2-by-4, 8 feet long
■ Lawn roller	■ 2-by-2, 6 feet long
■ Hopper	■ Two 1-by-2s, 3 feet long
■ Mechanical spreader	
■ Grass rake	
■ Garden hoe	
■ Grass plugger	
■ Tamper	

PREPARING THE BED

Smoothing the soil
Till the lawn bed, then rake it, removing stones and other debris. Check the grading and drainage around the house and in the rest of the yard *(pages 26-30)*, and make corrections if necessary. Test the soil and add amendments as needed *(pages 38-39)*; work them into the soil thoroughly. Rake the soil again to remove any remaining debris.

Firming the soil

Remove the filler plug on the barrel of a lawn roller and fill the barrel halfway with water in order to increase the roller's weight. Push the roller in parallel rows across the lawn bed to flatten it, then roll the area again, perpendicular to the first pass. Fill in any low spots revealed by rolling, rake the fill smooth, then roll the entire bed again.

Filler Plug

NEW GRASS FROM SEED

Sowing seed with a hopper

Measure the correct quantity of seed for the entire area *(chart, pages 265-266)*, then divide it into two equal portions. Do not try to speed growth by using more than the recommended quantity of seed. Walk slowly over the plot in parallel lines, scattering seed from the hopper by turning the crank steadily until you have covered the entire area once with half the seed; then, walking in rows at right angles to the first direction, sow the other half of the seed. For even coverage over a large area, use a mechanical spreader, following the same sowing pattern. Rake the area lightly with a grass rake to mix the seed into the soil, then roll it with a half-filled roller to ensure good contact between the seed and soil.

Covering and watering

Scatter clean straw over the seedbed, covering it so that half the soil can be seen beneath the straw. Mist the bed just enough to soak the soil without forming puddles or rivulets. Keep the soil dark with moisture until the seeds germinate—about 2 to 3 weeks, depending on the type of grass and the growing conditions—then water once a day until the seedlings are ½ inch tall. Thereafter, water as frequently as necessary to prevent the lawn from drying out. Do not mow or walk on the new grass until it is 3 inches high; at that point, either rake off the straw or leave it to decompose into the soil.

STARTING A LAWN WITH SPRIGS

Furrowing the soil

After preparing the bed *(pages 63-64)*, soak it with water and let it seep in for 24 hours. With the corner of a garden-hoe blade, cut a series of straight furrows 3 to 4 inches deep and 6 to 12 inches apart.

Grass Sprig

Setting the sprigs

Place sprigs in each furrow at 6- to 12-inch intervals, slanting them upward from the bottom of a furrow to the top of one side *(right)*. The closer they are planted, the faster the lawn will fill in. Press soil gently around the roots with your hands, leaving some blades of each sprig protruding above the ground. Smooth the soil and level it around the sprigs. When you have planted all of the sprigs, keep the lawn moist until they have rooted, then water them as you would a mature lawn.

PLANTING WITH PLUGS

Cutting holes for planting

Prepare the soil bed *(pages 63-64)*, soak it thoroughly, and let the water seep in for 24 hours before planting. Mark the placement of each plug hole, spacing them as recommended for your grass type. Use a grass plugger, available at a nursery or garden center, to make the holes. Press the foot bar down until it touches the ground, then twist the handle a quarter-turn. Lift the plugger, extracting a core of soil, then deposit the core on the ground.

A SPACING TOOL FOR PLUGS

Grass plugs should be planted in even rows 12 to 18 inches apart. You can mark a precise planting grid on your lot with the homemade spacing tool shown at right. To make one, drive 3½-inch nails through a 2-by-4 at whatever interval you have chosen, then attach a 6-foot-long 2-by-2, braced with two 3-foot-long 1-by-2s, to serve as a handle. Drag the tool the length of the plot to scratch parallel lines in the soil; pull it across the plot to complete the grid. Plant a plug at each intersection.

Planting the plugs

Fill the holes with water; allow it to drain completely. If your plugs are square *(photograph)*, round them gently with your hands to fit the holes. Then insert one plug in each hole. With the ball of your foot, step gently on each plug to bring it even with the surrounding soil. Break up the extracted soil cores with a garden rake. Using a grass rake, smooth the ground between plugs, erasing any footprints. Water the area daily for 2 weeks, then water every other day for a month until the plugs have rooted. Once the plugs are established, water and mow the lawn regularly to stimulate growth.

Grass Plug

INSTANT GREEN FROM ROLLS OF SOD

Laying the sod

Prepare the bed as directed on pages 63 and 64, making it 1 inch lower than any adjoining walkways, driveways, or patios. Wet the soil thoroughly a day or two before laying the sod, and keep the soil bed moist but not muddy while laying the rolls. Lay the first course of sod along a straight pavement or a staked string to provide a uniform edge. Unroll sod gently to avoid breaking off corners and edges. If a section feels uneven, roll it up and relevel the ground beneath it. For later courses, kneel on a piece of plywood or planking laid across the new sod to avoid creating depressions. Butt the sod rolls together as tightly as possible, staggering joints between them as shown above. At the end of a row, cut excess with a sharp knife *(inset)*, and use these pieces to fill oddly shaped areas around the perimeter of your lot.

Establishing root contact

Tamp the sod firmly against the soil bed; alternatively, roll the turf with an empty lawn roller. Water the new sod every day for 2 weeks; small pieces at the ends of rows may dry out more quickly than full sections and need more frequent watering. After 2 weeks, try to lift a piece of sod by the grass blades; if it has rooted, the blades will tear and you can begin watering less frequently. Otherwise, retamp the piece, continue watering daily, and test again in a few more days.

A Carpet of Ground Cover

Ground covers are excellent problem solvers. Many flourish in deep shade where grasses won't grow. Their wide range of color, foliage, and flowers can break up the monotony of open spaces or form a transition between low grasses and tall shrubs. And planting a hillside with ground cover eliminates the hazards of mowing on a slope, yet still prevents erosion.

PLANTING

Some ground covers can be grown from seed, but most are propagated either as cuttings taken from established plants or by dividing large plants into smaller ones, as described on pages 74-75. You can use these methods yourself if you have access to a patch of ground cover either in your own yard or that of a cooperative neighbor. Alternatively, ground covers are sold as immature plants in lots of 50 or more temporarily rooted in a shallow tray called a flat.

The chart on pages 267-269 provides a selection of ground cover plants including information on their special requirements. Consult your nursery about the number of plants of a particular variety you will need to cover a given area. And before planting, mulch the area with a layer of shredded pine bark to help keep weeds at bay. Even so, expect to weed often during the first year.

COPING WITH SLOPES

To prevent the rain from washing newly planted ground cover down an erosion-prone slope, you must stabilize the soil long enough for the ground cover to spread out. Jute netting, a loosely woven, biodegradable material, works especially well *(page 72)*. It does not restrict plant growth or prevent water and nutrients from reaching the roots. Within 6 to 9 months the netting starts to disintegrate, disappearing completely in about 2 years.

CONTROLLING EXPANSION

After ground covers have become established, they may run rampant. Keep varieties that spread by surface runners in check by pruning. Cut the runner with pruning shears no closer than three or four nodes—points where leaves attach to the stem—from the main stem. A species that widens its coverage by means of the root system can be temporarily contained by cutting the roots along the border of the bed *(page 75)*, but for a more permanent solution, install edging. Whenever ground cover begins to pop up in a lawn or flower bed, weed it out immediately before it grows beyond control.

TOOLS	MATERIALS
■ Garden trowel	■ Mulch
■ Hammer	■ Jute netting
■ 3-inch masonry trowel	■ Sod staples
■ Hand fork	■ Flat
■ Spade	■ Plant hormone powder
■ Weeding fork	■ Rooting medium
	■ Sheet of glass or clear plastic

A TECHNIQUE FOR PLANTING

Separating the plants

Remove no more than half a dozen plants and rooting medium from the flat.
Separate the plants with your fingers *(above)*, taking care not to injure the roots. Set
the plants in the ground immediately.

Setting the plants

To prepare a planting hole, push a garden trowel through the mulch and into the soil, then pull it toward you, opening a small pocket in the ground. Holding the soil back with the trowel, set a plant in the pocket, with about ¼ inch of its stem below ground level *(left)*. With the trowel, gently push the displaced soil back into the pocket.

Tamping the soil

Smooth the soil and mulch with your fingers, patting the mulch down around the stem, forming a slight depression to catch and hold moisture *(inset)*. Set in the remaining plants, and water them for at least half an hour with a lawn sprinkler or with a hose set for a fine mist. Continue to water the new plants every other day for a month.

STABILIZING A SLOPE

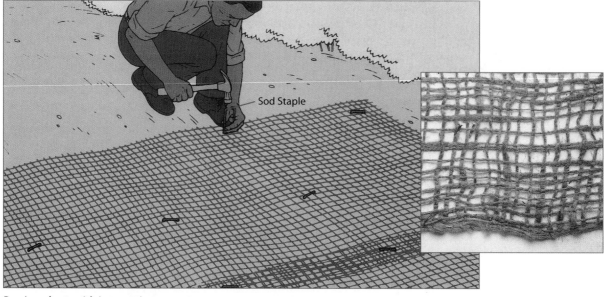

Sod Staple

Bracing plants with jute netting

Strip away any sod, grade the slope if necessary and prepare the soil for planting. Working uphill from the bottom of the slope, unroll strips of jute netting *(photograph)* across the incline. Overlap the strips 8 inches and secure them with sod staples *(above)*. Cover the area with an inch of mulch. With a 3-inch masonry trowel, dig holes for the plants in staggered rows to prevent water from washing straight down the hill. After setting the plants, mold a basin around the lower side of each stem with your hand to prevent runoff, then water.

PROPAGATION BY CUTTINGS

Obtaining a cutting

Cut a 3- to 6-inch length from a main stem or an entire side stem of a well-established plant. The stem should contain three to five nodes. With a small sharp knife, make a clean, slanting cut slightly below the nodes *(right)*.

Nodes

Preparing the cutting for planting

Pinch off any flowers or seed heads from the stem *(left)*; if allowed to remain, they will divert nutrients away from the roots that will form on the cutting. Trim the leaves from the bottom of the cutting so that no foliage will be buried in the planting. Allow the cut end of the stem to dry out slightly; if the leaves begin to wilt, place them on a damp towel.

Planting the cuttings

Fill a flat with a moistened rooting medium, such as a combination of sand and peat moss in equal parts, to about an inch from the top. With a stick or a pencil, poke holes in the medium just deep enough to cover two or three nodes on the cuttings. Dip the end of each cutting into plant hormone powder, available at nurseries or garden-supply outlets, to encourage root growth. Set the cutting in a hole and tamp rooting medium down around it. After planting all the cuttings, water the entire flat gently but thoroughly. Cover the flat with a sheet of glass or clear plastic to protect the young plants until they can survive outdoors. Keep them in a warm room and out of direct sunlight. When new leaves appear, the cuttings are ready to be transplanted *(page 71)*.

MULTIPLICATION BY DIVISION

Uprooting the plants

Water the plants well a couple of days before you divide them to soften the ground. Using a hand fork or a spading fork, dig around a clump of plants containing 8 to 12 new plants. Raise the clump and guide the roots away from the fork with your free hand *(right)*.

Separating the plants

Shake or rinse enough soil from the clump to reveal the roots, then carefully pull apart individual plants *(left)*. After discarding any wilted or yellowed plants, return two or three of the stems to the original hole, then set the rest in a new hole and water them thoroughly.

CONTROLLING THE SPREAD OF GROUND COVERS

Countering an invasion

For deep-rooting plants—pachysandra and ivy, for example—slice straight down into the soil along the edge of the ground cover bed with a sharp spade, penetrating to the full depth of the plants' roots, usually about 6 to 8 inches *(above, left)*. If ground cover begins to pop up in a lawn or flower bed, remove it by hand with a weeding fork. Hold the base of the ground cover with one hand as you push the blade down into the soil alongside the root *(above, right)*, then lever the plant out of the ground.

CHAPTER 3

Shrubs and Trees

Shrubs and their larger cousins, trees, create a variety of visual delights, but they have practical uses, too. Trees can shade a deck or patio; shrubs can serve as a living privacy fence, a border to walkways and flower beds, or a windscreen. Planting—or transplanting—shrubs and trees is not difficult, and with regular pruning and fertilizing, these stately specimens will provide a lifetime of enjoyment.

Having the tree this close to the fence may be awkward when it is larger. Be sure to consider the size of the mature tree before you plant.

The shrub gives visual weight and substance to this flower garden.

Mulching helps trees retain moisture and makes mowing easier, but mulch that touches the bark or forms a "volcano" mound can harm a tree.

Small, casual shrubs blend nicely with other plants for a low-maintenance, attractive landscape.

Trees and larger, more sculptured shrubs give this home an established, regal appearance.

Shrubs: Beautiful and Versatile

Shrubs are surely the most versatile of landscape elements. With a little training or trimming, they can add a variety of shapes and textures to the yard *(opposite)*.

BASIC SHRUB CARE

Throughout the spring and summer, give shrubs a long, slow watering every 2 weeks—every 7 to 10 days during dry spells. Fertilize them no later than the spring growth spurt; later applications stimulate new growth that will suffer in winter.

Spread shredded pine bark or other organic mulch around shrubs to insulate the roots against heat and cold, and to inhibit weeds. Renew mulch in the spring and fall.

THE VALUE OF PRUNING

Few tasks are more important than pruning. It eliminates damaged and diseased wood as well as crossing branches, which can abrade each other and leave the plant open to infection. Pruning also encourages new growth and boosts flower and fruit production. Finally, pruning keeps the shrub in bounds and shapes it.

Prune shrubs several times a year. In the spring, remove winter damage and do light trimming. Wait to prune shrubs such as azaleas, which flower on old wood, until the blossoms have wilted. Most other shrubs can be pruned through the winter and up to midspring—or in summer after flowering.

Summer calls for biweekly shapings and trimmings. After the shrubs have flowered, snip off one third of the older stems at ground level, so that each plant renews itself every 3 years or so.

WINTERIZING

Some shrubs need protection from wind, cold, and snow. A local nursery can tell you which plants need help through the winter. Effective methods of protecting shrubs are shown on page 86. For the best results, winterize shrubs before the first hard freeze.

Heavy, wet snow is especially damaging to evergreens. After a storm, dislodge snow gently, taking care not to snap the branches.

TOOLS	MATERIALS
■ Pruning shears	■ Mulch
■ Loppers	■ Fertilizer
■ Pruning saw	■ Burlap
■ Hedge trimmer	■ Twine
■ Hedge shears	■ 2-by-3s
■ Action hoe	■ 1-by-4s
■ Sprinkler extension	■ 3-inch nails
■ Sprinkler hose	■ Stakes and string
■ Staple gun	
■ Saw	
■ Hammer	

Border

Accents

Group

Hedge

Specimen

Using shrubs in a landscape

Depending on where they are planted and how they are combined, shrubs offer many landscaping options. Besides their visual appeal, shrubs can be living fences or screens for trash bins and compost heaps. In deciding what shrubs to plant and where, consider how they will look in relation to the house, as well as how they appear from indoors. Landscape architects call a single free-standing shrub selected for its color, shape, or seasonal blossoms a specimen.

Several shrubs differing in sizes and colors, perhaps combined with a tree, are known as a group. Shrubs strategically located to contrast with or complement an architectural feature are called accents. A closely spaced row of a single species forms a hedge, useful to define property lines and preserve privacy. A combination of trees and shrubs becomes an informal border, offering diverse and contrasting colors and textures.

PRUNING AND TRIMMING

Pruning to promote growth

To encourage a new branch *(dashed lines)* in a sparse area of a shrub, grasp a branch just below a lateral bud—that is, a bud pointing outward from the side of the branch. Hold a pair of pruning shears at a 45-degree angle and sever the branch about ¼ inch above the bud, taking care not to damage it *(inset)*.

Lateral Bud

Removing damaged wood

Cut back a broken or diseased branch to healthy wood, either at a point just beyond a lateral bud or flush with the nearest healthy stem *(left)*. After cutting branches from a diseased shrub, clean blades of shears or saw with alcohol to avoid infecting other plants.

Thinning for health and light

After the growing season each year, trim and shape the shrub's outer branches. Remove completely any branches that are weak or misshapen, or that cross other branches. Prune individual branches at a main stem, and main stems near the ground *(left)*. Then, to let sunlight reach new buds and foliage next spring, cut away up to one third of the oldest stems.

The right way to prune roses

Every fall—after the last bloom but well before the first frost—cut away deadwood, small shoots, and crossing branches. Then cut back every main branch by a third of its length *(above, left)*. In the spring, cut away any stems damaged by winter weather. Then prune all healthy branches back to the point where their stems are at least ⅜ inch thick *(above, right)*. The spring pruning should leave a compact, bowl-shaped bush. During the growing season, regularly trim away all dead and damaged wood, as well as small branches.

Trimming hedges

For a formal hedge, stretch a level string taut between posts at the ends of the hedge as a cutting guide. To speed the work, use an electric or battery-operated hedge trimmer held at the height of the string. Draw the trimmer across the hedge top, taking care not to poke the tip of the tool into the hedge. Alternatively, use hedge shears as shown in the inset. If any long shoots are growing into a gap in the hedge, cut the shoots back with pruning shears to stimulate thick growth that will fill the hole. Shape an informal, relatively irregular hedge as you would a shrub, using pruning shears and trying to create a natural, feathery appearance; take special care to prune out any branches that have grown faster than the others. Trim both formal and informal hedges narrower at the top than at the bottom, to permit sunlight to reach the base of the hedge. After trimming a hedge, shake it to dislodge the clippings, then rake them away.

ROUTINE CARE TO KEEP SHRUBS HEALTHY

Stirring up the soil

Cultivating the soil around a shrub bed makes weeding easier and watering more effective. Use an action hoe *(left)* to loosen weeds and break up compacted soil. Push the hoe blade about 2 inches into the earth—shallower if it catches the roots of a shrub—and work it back and forth parallel to the surface. After weeding the bed, use the hoe again to smooth the soil before watering or applying mulch.

Getting water to the roots

The best way to water specimens and small groups is with a sprinkler extension *(above, left)*. This wandlike device with a fine-spray nozzle allows you to direct water at the base of a shrub. For larger groups and hedges, surround the bed with a sprinkler hose *(above, right)*. Water shrubs for at least 10 minutes or until the soil is thoroughly saturated. Puddles on the ground indicate overwatering, which can damage the roots; stop watering immediately.

Spreading mulch

Twice a year, rake away old mulch from around shrubs and replace it with fresh material. In spring, spread an even layer of dense material, such as woodchips or ground-up bark, about 2 inches thick. Use only aged mulch—new chips and bark leach valuable nitrogen from the soil—and keep it away from stems; moisture in the mulch could encourage fungus, insect infestation, and root rot. Before the first frost, insulate the bed with 3 inches of pine needles or oak leaves.

COUNTERMEASURES AGAINST THE COLD

Protection from wind and snow

Before the first frost, cover low-growing shrubs with evergreen branches *(above, left)* or spread a double thickness of burlap over them and peg it to the ground. To shield taller shrubs that are exposed to the full force of the wind, build a shelter of stakes and burlap to the full height of the shrub *(above, center)*. First, drive several stakes in a tight circle all around the plant, then staple the burlap to the stakes. Wind twine around evergreens to prevent heavy, wet snow from weighing down the branches and breaking them. Loop the twine around the bottom of the shrub, then wrap it tightly enough to hold the branches upright *(above, right)*. At the top, tie the twine into another loop.

Shelter under an eave

A sloping shelter on a frame of 2-by-3s prevents snow that slides off a roof from damaging shrubs next to a house. Cut a pair of pointed 2-by-3 posts at least 2 feet longer than the height of the shrubs and drive them a foot or more into the ground next to the house. In front of the shrubs, drive posts 1 foot shorter than the posts erected next to the wall. Fasten 2-by-3 crossbars to each pair of posts, then nail a canopy of 1-by-4s on the crossbars as shown at right.

Crossbar

Putting Shrubs in New Places

Often, as a landscaping plan evolves and matures, the need to discard or transplant old shrubs and to plant new ones arises. Techniques for accomplishing these tasks are shown on these and the following pages.

TIMING AND PREPARATION

Moving an old shrub—or planting a new one—is best done in early spring or fall. A few days before transplanting a shrub, water it generously to soften the soil around its roots, then proceed as shown on the next page. Have a tarpaulin on hand to help move the shrub easily, and plastic sheeting to keep soil off the lawn.

BUYING FROM A NURSERY

Except for some flowering shrubs—rhododendron and laurel, for example—which can be propagated through a technique called layering *(page 94)*—new shrubs come most often from nurseries. The plants come in three forms: rooted in a ball of soil and wrapped in burlap; grown and rooted in plastic containers; and with bare roots.

SELECTING HEALTHY PLANTS

Choose shrubs suited to your climate and soil conditions *(see appendix)* and check their condition carefully. Sound, undamaged bark and bright foliage on well-shaped branches spaced evenly around the stem are signs of a hardy specimen. Reject plants that have broken branches, bruised bark, or pale leaves, or those that are growing in dry soil.

Ask a nursery worker to show you the roots of container-grown plants. Look for a thick profusion of roots at the rootball's bottom; reject a shrub with roots that coil around the rootball or protrude from the top—sure signs of being potbound. In a healthy burlapped shrub, the rootball has a firm, solid feeling, with moist soil and no weeds. Bare-root stock should be undamaged, clean smelling, and uniform in color.

Plant shrubs immediately if possible, or store them in shade and keep the roots moist; if you cannot plant a bare-rooted shrub within a week, bury it in a shallow trench and keep it watered until you can plant it permanently.

TOOLS	MATERIALS
■ Pruning shears	■ Plastic sheeting
■ Mattock	■ Twine
■ Spade	■ Tarpaulin
■ Digging bar	■ Burlap
■ Garden fork	■ Peat moss
■ Garden trowel	■ Sand
	■ Fertilizer
	■ Rooting powder

SAFETY TIP

Shrubs are heavy; lift with the arms and legs and wear a back brace to reduce risk of back strain. Gloves protect your hands during spade work.

DISCARDING AN UNWANTED PLANT

Digging out the roots

Cut off most of the shrub's outer branches with pruning shears and trim main stems to a length of 2 or 3 feet. With a mattock, dig a trench around the shrub 1 foot or more from the stem and extending down through the root system. Undercut the shrub with a spade or digging bar to sever all the roots, then pull out the shrub by the trunk.

Refilling the hole

Knock the soil off the roots and into the hole with a spade or garden fork. If the plant is diseased, spread plastic sheeting in the hole to collect the soil and dispose of it away from the yard and garden. Refill the hole with soil and tamp it firmly. Add more soil to form a loose mound 4 to 6 inches high; the soil will settle in a few months, leaving the area level.

RELOCATING A SHRUB

Defining the rootball

Wrap the plant with twine to gather the branches into a compact bundle. Score the ground with the point of a shovel or spade to mark a circle roughly the diameter of the wrapped plant; this defines the size of the rootball. Make another circle about 9 inches outside the first.

Cutting out the rootball

Lay a canvas tarpaulin or sheet of heavy plastic next to the outside circle to receive the soil. Dig out the soil between the two circles to the depth of the shrub's main roots, usually about 18 inches. Undercut the rootball all around the plant with the spade or shovel, freeing it.

Wrapping the rootball

Cut a square sheet of natural-fiber, biodegradable burlap about 3 times the diameter of the rootball and place it next to the hole; do not use synthetic fabric or plastic. Push against one side of the rootball to tip the shrub on its side and stuff at least half of the burlap under the tilted rootball *(above, left)*. For large shrubs, consider enlisting a helper. Tip the ball toward the opposite side of the hole, then pull the burlap from under the ball *(above, right)*, roughly centering the ball on the burlap square. Lift the edges of the burlap and tie them securely around the stem with twine.

Pulling out the shrub

Set a sheet of canvas or heavy plastic next to the hole and lift the shrub onto the sheet. You may need a helper to assist in moving medium-sized or larger shrubs. Carry or slide the shrub on the sheet to its new location. Before replanting, unwrap the branches but leave the rootball in the burlap. Cut away any broken branches and prune the shrub by about a third to compensate for any roots lost through digging it up. Refill the old hole with soil.

PLANTING A BALLED AND BURLAPPED SHRUB

Digging the hole

At the new location, dig a circular hole about twice as wide and half again as deep as the rootball. Pile the soil on a plastic or canvas sheet next to the hole.

Conditioning the soil

Add peat moss and other amendments to the soil that was removed. Blend the soil and other materials thoroughly, keeping the mixture on the sheet and off grass or ground cover. Soil recipes: For loamy soil, add one part peat moss to two parts soil; for clay soil, add one part peat moss and one part sand to one part soil. For sandy soil, mix equal amounts of peat moss and soil. To any of these mixtures, add slow-release fertilizer in the amount recommended on the package.

Making a base for the shrub

Shovel a layer of the conditioned soil into the hole and compact it with your feet or a tamper. Repeat the process, partially filling the hole to a depth about 2 inches shallower than the height of the rootball.

Positioning the shrub

Set the shrub in the hole, adjusting the bottom as needed to make the main stem vertical. Lay a straight stick across the hole to make sure the top of the rootball is about 2 inches above ground level. If the shrub sits too high or too low, lift it out of the hole and add or remove conditioned soil to bring the shrub to the right height. Add soil mixture to the hole around the rootball, tamping as you go, until the hole is two-thirds full. Then loosen the burlap and spread it over the soil mixture *(inset)*. Fill the hole with water, and let it seep into the ground. Then add soil mixture to about 1 inch above ground level and tamp it down firmly.

Forming a basin of soil

Build a soil dam about 4 inches high around the planting hole to catch water for the shrub. Fill this basin with water and let it seep into the soil. Spread a 2-inch layer of mulch or bark chips around the shrub. Cover the basin walls but stop 2 inches short of the main stem. Keep the soil moist around the transplanted shrub for the first few months, but do not overwater.

PROPAGATING SHRUBS BY LAYERING

Wounding the branch

In early spring, bend a healthy lower branch to touch the ground about 12 inches from the tip and dig a bowl-shaped hole about 6 inches deep there. Bend the branch into the hole. Where it touches the center of the hole, slit the branch diagonally about halfway through with a sharp knife and wedge a twig in the cut *(inset)*. Sprinkle the wound with rooting powder, a synthetic hormone available at garden centers.

Anchoring the branch

Mix enough topsoil, peat moss, and sand, in equal parts, to fill the hole, then put about one fourth of the mixture into the hole. Bend the branch back into the hole with the cut facing down and cover it with soil mix. Anchor the branch with a pair of crossed sticks *(left)*, and fill the hole with the remaining soil mix, making sure that 6 inches of the branch protrude above ground level. Water the soil mix thoroughly and set a rock over the crossed sticks to hold them in place.

Separating the new shrub

Do not disturb the branch until next spring, then dig it up. Pull away some soil to see if roots have developed at the cut. If three to five roots are present, sever the branch to free the new plant from the old one *(right)*; if not, rebury the branch and check again in the fall. After detaching the branch, push gently on the rootball to slant the roots in the opposite direction from the tip. Plant the newly propagated shrub as you would any other, tilting the rootball so that the top of the plant points upward.

Keeping Trees in Good Health

Like the houses they protect and adorn, trees need regular care, sometimes by professionals. You can perform the routine chores of low-level pruning, fertilizing, and pest control, but tasks such as bracing limbs with guy wires, or climbing to a high perch to cut them off, should be left to a specialist.

THE RIGHT WAY TO PRUNE

Judicious pruning can improve a tree's health. But because each cut wounds the tree, you can also do harm if you prune carelessly.

A tree walls off a wounded area with cells and chemical barriers that keep disease-causing organisms from invading healthy tissue. These guardians develop at the base of each branch in a swollen area called the branch collar.

Part of the collar is destroyed by pruning a branch flush to the trunk, a method favored in the past; the wound closes slowly, if at all. Cutting too far from the trunk is also a poor practice, since the stub is too far from the source of protective cells. To close properly, cuts must be made at a precise angle, just outside the collar *(page 99)*. Leave the wound untreated, or apply a thin coat of asphalt-based tree paint. Other paints retard closure.

Do your pruning in late winter or early spring, before the buds open. Prune flowering trees just after the blooms fade, and remove any broken or diseased branches from all trees immediately.

FEEDING TREES

To maintain normal growth, trees need a variety of nutrients, often provided in the form of fertilizer. Among the most effective fertilizers are organic materials such as cottonseed meal, bone meal, or blood meal.

Fertilizer works best when it is spread on the ground or injected as a liquid *(pages 102-103)*. You can also spray liquid fertilizer onto a tree's leaves *(page 104)*, or hammer fertilizer spikes around the drip line *(page 102)*. However, if the drip line is 30 inches or less from the trunk, do not use spikes.

The best time to apply fertilizer is in late autumn, when all the leaves have fallen and trees begin storing nutrients for the winter. You can also fertilize in early spring; for flowering trees, wait until they begin to bloom.

Whatever season you choose, avoid overuse of fertilizer. One or two applications a year is enough for young trees, and once every 3 to 5 years for mature ones.

SAFE PEST CONTROL

If a tree looks sickly or harbors bugs you do not recognize, call your local extension service for a diagnosis. The prescription is likely to be a spray-on chemical, which must be handled with care. You can safely spray a tree up to 25 feet tall with the equipment shown on page 104. Hire a professional to treat larger trees.

Before you start, check local laws governing chemical spraying and study the instructions on the package label. Some pesticides must be mixed with water; dilute them exactly as directed. Wear protective clothing and keep children and pets out of the area.

If you prefer a nontoxic treatment, try dormant oil, a commercial mixture of mineral oil and water. Sprayed on a tree in early spring before leaves emerge, it coats and smothers aphids, scales, and mites, even before they hatch from eggs. Read the directions on the label carefully. Although harmless to humans, the oil can damage evergreens and certain species of beech, birch, and maple.

Another nontoxic approach is biological control, using a pest's natural enemies. A single ladybug, for example, can eat four dozen aphids a day, while a bacterium called Bt attacks gypsy-moth and other caterpillars but is harmless to other organisms. Ask your nursery operator or extension agent about pest fighters indigenous to your area.

TOOLS

- Pruning shears
- Lopping shears
- Pole shears
- Pruning saw
- Broadcast or trough spreader
- Root-zone injector
- Spray canister
- Garden-hose sprayer

MATERIALS

- Dry fertilizer
- Tree spikes
- Fertilizer cartridges
- Liquid fertilizer
- Pesticide

SAFETY TIP

Wear gloves when handling fertilizers. Add goggles when cutting tree branches. Follow manufacturer's instructions precisely when spraying pesticides. Depending on toxicity, you may need to don not only gloves and goggles but boots, long sleeves, and a dust mask or cartridge respirator, as well.

THE ART OF PRUNING

The basic guidelines

Well-formed young trees have a straight central branch, or leader, extending from the top; the main limbs have U-shaped crotches evenly distributed around the trunk at least a foot apart vertically. To maintain this strong, balanced framework, prune away any undesirable features: Remove branches having a tight, V-shaped crotch, which makes a weak joint. Cut off suckers or water sprouts—which can grow anywhere on a tree and have no lateral branches—as well as any buds from which new suckers and water sprouts might grow. Dispose of branch stubs, dead or broken limbs, and small branches that grow toward the trunk or across larger limbs; crossover growth can damage the trunk and other branches by rubbing against them. Periodically thin inner branches of mature trees to admit light. On deciduous trees, remove low limbs that keep you from walking under the tree. Leave the lower limbs on evergreens in place.

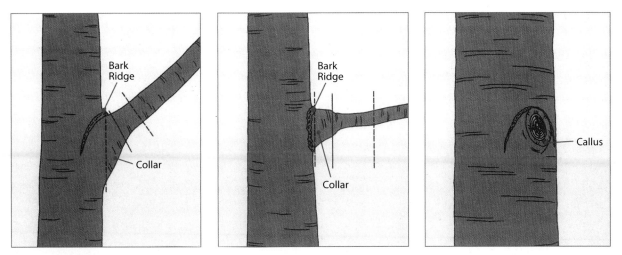

Proper pruning cuts

Two features of a branch govern the position and angle of a pruning cut—the thick collar at the base of the branch and the dark ridge in the bark of the parent branch or trunk. On mature deciduous trees, trim branches off square near the collar *(solid line, above left)*. Do not cut into the collar or the ridge, and do not leave a stub *(dotted lines)*. A branch on a very young deciduous tree or an evergreen may have a large collar and a bark ridge that encircles the base *(above, center)*. Prune just outside the collar and parallel to the bark ridge *(solid line)*, neither leaving a stub nor cutting into the ridge or the collar *(dotted lines)*. In a year or so, a hard callus should form at the edge of the wound *(above, right)*, later closing over the cut.

THREE TOOLS FOR SMALL BRANCHES

Shearing small sprouts

Use pruning shears to sever buds and small branches that are up to ¼ inch thick. Cut as close to the trunk as you can without damaging the bark.

Cutting off small branches

To remove a branch up to 1 inch thick, set the cutting blade of a pair of lopping shears on top of the limb, with the side of the blade against the trunk or supporting branch. Angle the lower blade away from the bark ridge and the collar, and bring the handles of the shears together in a single smooth motion. Do not twist the shears or use them to tear the branch from the tree. If the shears do not make a clean cut on the first attempt, sharpen them or switch to a saw.

Extendable shears

Pole shears can cut branches as big as 1 inch in diameter and reach branches up to 15 feet overhead. The pole consists of a telescoping plastic or wooden shaft. A cutting blade under a stationary hook is operated by a cord that runs through a pulley to increase leverage *(photograph)*. Place the hook over the base of the branch in the position shown here. Wrap the cord once around the pole to keep the shaft from bowing, and pull the cord sharply. Cut close enough to the branch collar so no stub remains. If the severed branch hangs in the tree, pull it down with the head of the shears, taking care not to break other branches.

SAWING OFF A LIMB

Removing the branch

When cutting a branch that is up to 3 inches thick, first trim off any secondary limbs. This will serve to lighten the branch and keep it from catching in the tree as it falls. Use a pruning saw to cut halfway through the bottom of the branch, about a foot from the trunk; this cut will stop bark from tearing loose when the branch falls. About an inch outside the first cut, saw through the branch from the top. When this second cut is halfway through the branch, the limb will snap off, leaving a stub.

Trimming the stub

For the third cut, saw 1 inch into the underside of the stub, just outside the branch collar and at a right angle to the stub. Make the fourth cut at the crotch of the stub, just outside the bark ridge at the base of the stub *(right)*. Support the stub with one hand and saw downward to meet the third cut.

FEEDING ROOTS FROM THE SURFACE

Mapping for surface fertilizer

Lay a string or garden hose around the tree at the drip line, which is directly below the tree's outermost leaves. Mark a second circle about two-thirds of the way in from the drip line to the center, but not less than 5 feet from the trunk. Mark a third circle about twice the drip-line distance from the trunk *(inset)*. Using a broadcast or trough spreader, spread tree fertilizer over the area between the inner- and outermost circles.

Placing tree spikes

Mark the drip line of your tree as for surface fertilizer, above. For each inch of trunk diameter, drive a spike into the ground along the drip line. Space the spikes evenly, and while hammering, shield the tops with the protective plastic cap provided.

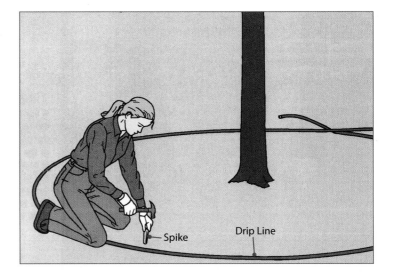

INJECTING FERTILIZER BY WATER PRESSURE

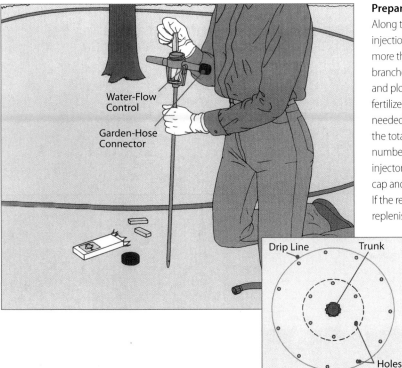

Water-Flow Control

Garden-Hose Connector

Preparing a root-zone injector

Along the tree's drip line *(opposite)*, mark spots for an injection every 2 to 3 feet. For a tree having a trunk more than 4 inches in diameter and widespread branches, mark a second circle halfway to the trunk and plot injector locations along it *(inset)*. Consult the fertilizer box for the number of fertilizer cartridges needed for each inch of tree trunk diameter. Divide the total by the number of injection points to get the number of cartridges per injection. Load the root-zone injector for one injection by unscrewing the reservoir cap and dropping in water-soluble fertilizer cartridges. If the reservoir is too small for all of them at one time, replenish the supply as the fertilizer dissolves.

Drip Line   Trunk

Holes

Using the injector

Close the water-flow control valve and connect a garden hose to the injector. Turn the water on to a medium flow, and open the control valve on the injector just enough to permit water to trickle out of the tube. Slowly push the tube into the soil, twisting it back and forth until it reaches a depth of 6 to 8 inches. In hard ground, allow the water to soften the dirt and ease the way. For trees with shallow roots, set the control valve halfway between OFF and HALF ON; for more deeply rooted trees, set it to HALF ON; for very large, well-established trees, start at HALF ON, then turn the valve to ON after the first minute. Leave the injector in place until the fertilizer has dissolved, then turn the water off, pull out the tube, and move to the next injection spot.

A HAND-PUMPED SPRAYER FOR SMALL JOBS

A pressurized canister

To fill the canister, remove the pump assembly. Pour liquid fertilizer or pesticide into a small amount of water in the canister, then add the rest of the water needed to dilute the chemical. Mix powdered chemicals thoroughly with the full measure of water in a bucket before pouring it into the canister. Screw in the pump, and vigorously raise and lower the handle several times to pressurize the tank. Aim the nozzle upward and squeeze the pistol grip to saturate the undersides of leaves. Adjust the fineness of the spray, if necessary, by turning the nozzle tip, and repressurize the tank whenever the spray weakens.

Pistol Grip

Pressure-Pump Handle

USING A GARDEN-HOSE SPRAYER

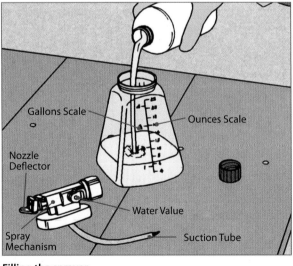

Gallons Scale

Ounces Scale

Nozzle Deflector

Water Value

Spray Mechanism

Suction Tube

Filling the sprayer

Pour concentrated liquid fertilizer or pesticide into the reservoir, using the ounces scale on its side to measure the desired amount. Add water slowly while watching the gallons scale, stopping when the mixture reaches the level that matches the amount of spray solution you need. Screw on the spray mechanism, close the water valve, and gently shake the sprayer.

Using the sprayer

Connect the sprayer to a garden hose and open the spigot. With the sprayer pointed at the tree, open the water valve; when spraying dormant oil, saturate both the trunk and the limbs. To control the force of the spray, turn the garden-hose spigot. Direct the spray upward with the nozzle deflector. Doing so allows you to keep the sprayer level enough for the suction tube to siphon chemicals into the spray.

How to Move a Tree

A tree's size, weight, and stability make it seem a permanent part of the landscape, but there are times when it is necessary to move a tree. Small or young trees, for example, may need to be temporarily stored out of the way of construction projects. And some trees should be permanently moved away from areas with poor drainage, unfavorable soil conditions, or extreme wind. Mature trees in good health can also be relocated to fit a new landscape plan.

A MATTER OF SIZE

In general, those trees up to 10 feet tall with trunks up to 3 inches thick can be moved with relative ease and can be expected to thrive after the experience. Larger trees, however, are unwieldy and are more vulnerable to shock; the job of moving them should be evaluated—and usually performed—by a professional.

PLANNING AHEAD

The best time to move a deciduous tree is late autumn or early spring, when the tree is dormant. An evergreen can be moved at any time. Several months to a year in advance, cut about half of the horizontal roots, but not the vertical taproot. Make these cuts in three 60-degree arcs 24 to 30 inches from the trunk *(page 106)*.

Pruning the tree *(pages 98-101)* in advance lessens the danger of shock by allowing new feeder roots time to form before the tree is moved. To compensate for the lost root capacity, however, prune away about a third of the branches.

TOOLS	MATERIALS
■ Spade	■ Burlap
■ Shovel	■ Twine
■ Rake	■ Mulch

SAFETY TIP

Wear work gloves when digging and a back brace to reduce the chance of injury when moving heavy objects such as trees.

Pruning the roots
Using a spade with a well-sharpened blade, sever the roots in a circle 24 to 30 inches wide around the trunk, recutting roots where they were pruned in advance. Push the blade into the ground at about a 30-degree angle toward the trunk (*dotted line*), so that the rootball will taper.

Earlier Pruning

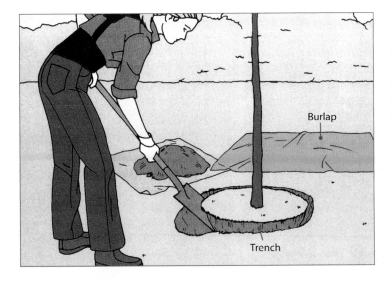

Uprooting the tree

Excavate an access trench, 18 inches deep, around the rootball. Thrust the blade of a spade—the long-handled variety works best—under the tree to sever the taproot and any other uncut roots *(left)*. With a helper, lift the tree by the rootball and place it on a square of burlap. Removing a tree with low branches may be easier if you work the burlap under the rootball before lifting the tree from the hole.

Burlap

Trench

Bagging the rootball

Draw the burlap up around the ball on all sides, twisting the excess around the trunk. Run twine around the ball in several directions, tilting the tree to get the string under it. When you have bound the rootball into a neat package, wrap the twine around the trunk several times and tie it off.

Storing the tree

If you can replant the tree within a week, set it in a shady spot, cover the rootball with mulch, and water it. To store a tree for longer periods, dig a hole about half the rootball depth in a shady area, protected from wind. Tip the rootball into the hole and cover it with a 6-inch layer of mulch *(above)*. Keep the rootball moist.

The Right Way to Plant a Tree

Trees are available for planting in three forms: balled and burlapped, container grown, or bare rooted. Before buying any young tree, however, use the charts on pages 270 to 281 to find out which species thrive in your area. Prepare a soil mixture for the planting hole as you would for a shrub *(page 92)*.

PLANTING A TREE

Bare-rooted trees, usually sold by mail-order nurseries, are generally smaller, younger, and less expensive than the others. Start such trees in the early spring, within a day or two of their arrival. The technique for setting a bare-rooted tree into the ground appears on the next page.

You can plant container-grown and balled and burlapped trees at any time of the year. A balled and burlapped tree is planted exactly as a similarly packaged shrub—as is a container-grown tree, once you have slipped the plastic pot from around the rootball as described opposite.

CARE AFTER PLANTING

Unless the tree has been container grown or pruned at the nursery, cut away about one-third of the branches *(pages 98-101)*. Wrap a plastic tree protector around the base of the trunk to prevent damage to the lower bark *(page 110)*.

Brace or guy trees in areas where high winds or playing children may loosen their roots *(page 111)*. Never tie braces or guy wires taut; root systems strengthen faster when a tree can sway gently in the wind. Guying kits are available at garden centers. You can assemble a tree brace yourself using galvanized wire and pieces of old garden hose.

Finally, water a newly planted tree well; it needs the equivalent of an inch of rainfall a week during the growing season.

TOOLS	MATERIALS
■ Utility knife	■ Tree protector
■ Pruning shears	■ 2-by-2 stakes
■ Spade	■ Cloth strips
■ 4-pound maul	■ Old garden hose
	■ Galvanized wire

CONTAINER-GROWN SPECIMENS

Trees from plastic pots
Slide the pot off the rootball, tapping or flexing the sides of the pot as necessary to loosen it. If the tree you buy has circling roots *(left)*, gently unwind them. Cut off large curling and matted roots with pruning shears. With a utility knife or sharp kitchen knife, score the rootball 1 inch deep from top to bottom in four or five locations that are evenly spaced *(inset)*. Plant the tree as shown for shrubs on pages 91-93.

TREES WITH BARE ROOTS

Positioning the roots
Dig a planting hole *(page 91)* about one and a half times as deep as the length of the tree's longest root; make the hole about as wide as it is deep. Pile soil in the center of the hole, then gently spread the tree roots over the mound. With a straight board as a guide *(right)*, adjust the mound so the soil-level mark on the tree trunk falls no lower than ground level.

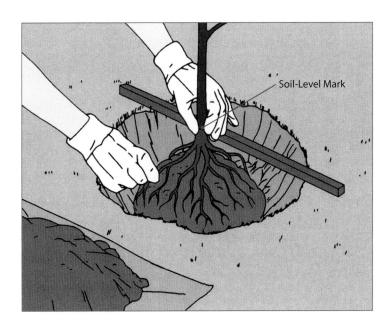

Soil-Level Mark

Filling in around the roots

Holding the tree vertically, scoop soil into the hole. Pack the soil gently but firmly around the roots to eliminate air pockets. Fill the hole two-thirds with soil, one-third with water. After the water has seeped away, add soil to ground level. Build a soil basin as shown on page 93, fill it with water, then mulch.

CARING FOR RECENT TRANSPLANTS

Protecting tender bark

Push back the soil at the tree trunk's base to a depth of about 2 inches. Coil a plastic tree protector around the trunk *(right)*. After installing the protector, slide it to the base of the tree. Replace the loosened soil. Tree protectors are designed to expand as the plant grows. At least once a year, check the protector for binding and loosen it as needed. Remove the protector after 2 to 3 years.

Tree Protector

Bracing small trees

For a trunk less than 3 inches thick, position a pair of 6-foot, 2-by-2 stakes next to the planting hole. With a 4-pound maul, drive them at least 18 inches into the ground. Tie one end of a cloth strip near the top of one post. Loop the cloth once around the trunk, leaving about 1 inch of slack. Tie the other end of the cloth to the second post, again leaving an inch of slack. Remove the bracing when the tree is firmly rooted—no later than a year after planting.

Guying a tree

For trunks 3 inches or more in diameter, drive three notched stakes into the ground outside the planting hole. Thread the end of a guy wire through a 1-foot-long length of garden hose. Loop the hose around the trunk above a branch, then twist the wire around itself to secure the hose to the tree. Tie the other end of the wire to the notch in a stake. Add two more guy wires, then adjust all three of them to allow the tree to sway slightly.

CHAPTER 4

Patios of Brick and Concrete

Masonry surfaces actually float on the surface of the ground, rising and subsiding with spring thaws and winter frosts. In the case of concrete, the slab floats on a layer of gravel, while bricks and stone embedded in sand shift individually to adapt to changing contours. Either structure requires considerable excavation, heavy work lightened by a rotary tiller used to loosen soil for easier removal.

Herringbone is one of many attractive brick patterns you can use to create a welcoming path or patio.

Consider using the same material that composes your path or patio to construct a raised flowerbed.

Using an accent color for the edge of a patio or path provides a clean visual line that emphasizes the geometry of its design.

Patterns to Set in Sand or Mortar

A patio with a surface of bricks or concrete paving blocks is weather-resistant and enduring. Because the brick or concrete pavers are small and uniform in size, such a patio is also easy to install and maintain.

THE SPECTRUM OF MATERIALS

Standing water and changing temperatures are tough on brick patios; buy paving bricks, which are stronger than those used to build vertical structures. As shown opposite, you can combine them in a number of patterns. Molded concrete paving blocks, on the other hand, are designed to interlock.

SAFETY TIP

Wear hard-toed shoes when you are transporting brick or concrete pavers. If you are working with mortar, leather-palmed work gloves will protect your hands from irritants.

CHOOSING SAND OR CONCRETE:

Both brick and concrete pavers may be set on a tightly compacted bed of sand *(pages 122-126)* or on a concrete slab with mortar *(page 127)*. Sand is self-draining and lets the pavers move independently as the earth shifts, and pavers set on sand can be leveled or replaced individually. Patios of mortared bricks or blocks, however, last longer, need less upkeep, and rarely have weeds.

MAINTAINING THE PATIO

Whether the pavers are on sand or concrete, moss may be a problem. Although it can be attractive, moss can also be a slippery hazard. To eliminate it, apply moss killer, sold at garden-supply stores. If your patio develops mildew stains, scrub it with household bleach. Finally, weeds can grow between pavers laid on sand, even when a weed-control barrier has been placed underneath. If that happens, you may need to spray all gaps with herbicide, taking care not to spray near trees and other desirable plants.

PAVERS FOR PATIOS

Brick pavers

The paving brick at near right measures about 3⅝ inches wide by 7⅝ inches long; these dimensions allow for ample mortar joints between bricks. You can also purchase paving bricks like the one above it, which is exactly twice as long as it is wide. For use on a sand bed, these bricks fit together without gaps to help keep weeds from poking through. In climates where the ground freezes, use paving bricks that are rated SX, which means they can withstand severe weather.

4" × 8"

3⅝" × 7⅝"

Concrete pavers
Molded concrete paving blocks come in numerous shapes; the three shown at left are among the more common. Because the blocks are laid down in interlocking patterns, they are less likely to shift position during or after installation.

OPTIONS WITH BRICK

Stack Bond

Running Bond

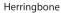

Basket Weave

Herringbone

An emphasis on regularity

You can set rectangular bricks in any of the four classic patterns shown above, or combine the patterns to give varied surface designs. Avoid the stack-bond arrangement for large patios, since it is difficult to align; instead, frame other patterns with a stack-bond border. A running-bond pattern, in which the bricks are staggered, is easier to lay uniformly over a broad area. Interlocking patterns like basket weave and herringbone, in which brick orientation varies, increase the durability of a sand-bed patio, since each brick is held in place by its neighbors. The basket weave above has brick faces exposed; another version has the bricks set on their sides, three to a square. Herringbone, with its directional nature, is useful for directing a viewer's eye to a particular spot.

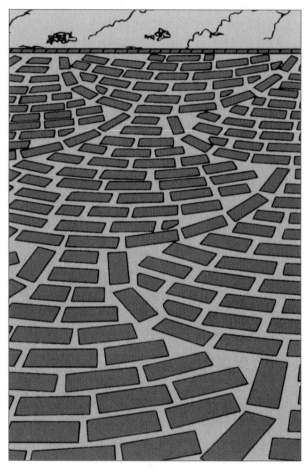

Layouts based on circles.
To accommodate a tree, a fountain, or other fixed object, lay a circular pattern *(above, left)*. Begin at the center with two rings of half bricks, then add rings of full-size bricks to fill an area of any size

(page 124). A scalloped effect like that used on European boulevards *(above, right)* is achieved with overlapping arcs of brick as shown on page 126. Loosely fill the scallops with whole and half bricks.

Bricks without Mortar

By far the easiest patio to build is one made of bricks set into a bed of sand. A sand base allows rainwater to seep down to tree or shrub roots, and sand lets bricks accommodate the earth below as it settles or shifts with freezing and thawing.

When planning a patio, consider the stability of the ground. Recent landfill more than 3 feet deep or water found within 1 foot of the surface may cause settling problems. If such conditions exist—or if you live in an earthquake zone—consult a landscape architect.

LAYING OUT A SAND BED

To minimize brick cutting, lay a dry run around the patio perimeter before excavating, adjusting the patio dimensions to incorporate as many whole bricks as possible. Be sure to plan for a permanent edging *(page 122)*, required to keep sand-laid bricks from shifting. Chop out tree roots near the surface that would prevent bricks from lying flat. Before digging, check with a building inspector to see if you must erect a silt fence to keep eroded soil on your property.

DRAINAGE

Usually, 2 inches of sand on well-tamped earth offers adequate drainage. Dense clay soils or heavy rainfall, however, often require the added drainage of a 4-inch layer of gravel under the sand. Use the estimator on page 128 to figure the amounts you need. To prevent sand from sifting down into the gravel, cover it with 15-pound roofing felt or 6-mil polyethylene sheeting punctured to let rainwater through. If drainage is a particular problem, slope the sand bed away from the house about 1 inch every 4 to 6 feet. Perforated drain tile or plastic tubing laid in the gravel layer helps drain water away from wet spots.

CHOOSING THE RIGHT BRICKS

Untextured, exterior-grade bricks are best; rough or grooved surfaces collect water that can crack bricks when it freezes. But avoid glazed bricks, which become slippery when wet. "Bricks" of molded concrete, which come in a wide array of colors and shapes, offer an alternative to traditional clay brick.

WITH GAPS OR WITHOUT

Patterns of bricks laid tight against one another control weeds better than bricks laid with gaps between them. For a gapless patio, buy special paving bricks exactly half as wide as they are long.

Other paving bricks are sized for mortar joints between them. The gap both accentuates the pattern and channels rainwater down the long side of the brick—away from the house, if you align the long edges with any slope the site may have. Plastic sheeting laid on the sand bed before the bricks are laid helps keep weeds from growing in the gaps, and sand swept into the gaps keeps the bricks from moving.

TWO METHODS FOR CUTTING BRICKS

Maul

Brickset

TOOLS

- Brickset
- 4-pound maul
- Mason's hammer
- Rubber mallet
- Level
- Framing square
- Circular saw with a carbide masonry blade

MATERIALS

- Bricks
- Washed gravel (¾-inch)
- Polyethylene sheeting
- Sand
- 2-by-2 stakes
- String

CAUTION

Before excavating, establish the locations of underground obstacles such as electric, water, and sewer lines, and dry wells, septic tanks, and cesspools.

SAFETY TIP

Wear eye protection when cutting bricks. A dust mask is recommended when trimming brick with a circular saw. Gloves help prevent blisters and abrasions.

Using a brickset

To cut a small number of bricks, use a wide chisel—called a brickset—and a 4-pound maul. Draw a cutting line on the brick, then cushion the brick on sand or a board. Hold the brickset vertically with the beveled edge facing away from you and strike the tool sharply. Then tilt the brickset slightly toward you and strike again, thus splitting the brick. Practice on a few broken bricks before you cut the bricks you will use.

Scoring bricks with a circular saw

Large numbers of bricks are more easily cut with the help of a circular saw fitted with a carbide masonry blade. Hold the brick in a simple jig made of 2-by-4 scraps, spaced a brick's width apart and nailed to a piece of plywood. Set the saw for a ¼-inch cut, then slowly guide the blade along the cutting line, grooving the brick. Make a matching groove on the other side, then hold the brick in your hand and break off the unwanted portion with the blunt end of a mason's hammer *(inset)*.

Mason's Hammer

EXCAVATING FOR A PATIO

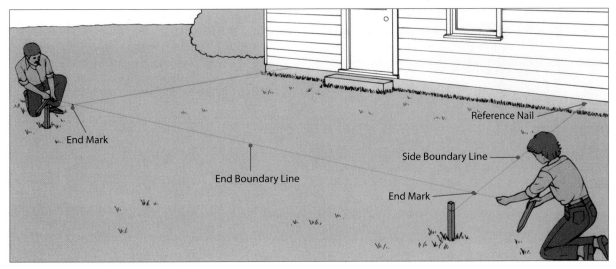

Laying out a rectangular site

Drive reference nails into the wall of the house to mark both sides of the patio. Use the method shown on page 130 to establish positions for 2-by-2 stakes opposite the nails and 2 feet beyond the end of the future patio. Tie string between the nails and stakes to establish side boundary lines for the patio and mark each string where the patio will end. With a helper *(above)*, stake a third string so that it crosses the marks you made on the side boundary lines. To excavate the area, first dig a trench along the boundary lines. Make the trench deep enough to accommodate the bricks, sand, and gravel if any. Work in parallel rows, back and forth between the perimeter trenches.

Laying out an irregular shape

Draw the patio on graph paper, with each square representing 1 square foot. To estimate the area of the patio, assign a rough fractional value to parts of squares inside the outline. Then add up the full squares and the fractions. Use this figure when buying brick, sand, and gravel. Lay out a garden hose in the shape of the patio, then outline the perimeter on the ground with a dispenser of powdered chalk. Trench around the perimeter, then excavate.

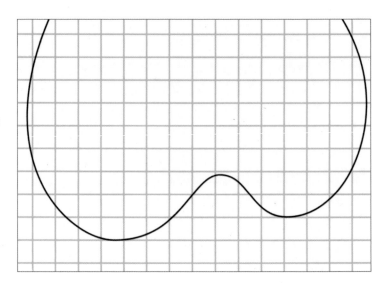

LAYING BRICKS IN SAND

Edging the perimeter

First, compact the earth inside the excavation with a tamper. Around the perimeter, dig a narrow trench such that the top of a brick stood on end in the trench will be even with the patio surface. (If a side of the patio will border a flower bed, let the edging extend 2 inches higher.) Tamp the bottom of the trench with the end of a 2-by-4, then stretch reference strings as guides for aligning the tops of the edging bricks with one another. Next, stand bricks upright around the perimeter (left), with their top edges touching the strings. Press earth against the bricks to hold them up. Add washed gravel as necessary, distributing it evenly over the surface with a rake. Cover the gravel with roofing felt, or polyethylene sheeting that has been punctured with drainage holes at 4- to 6-inch intervals. Spread a 2-inch layer of sand over the bed. Dampen the sand, then tamp the surface again.

ALTERNATIVE EDGINGS

To make a sawtooth pattern with teeth protruding 2 inches above the patio surface *(above)*, set the bricks at an angle of 45° in the trench. Other choices for edgings include rot-resistant redwood or pressure-treated 2-by-6s *(above, right)* set in a narrower trench, or upright bricks set in a curve *(right)* for a rounded corner. To lay out a curved corner, use a level to align the tops of the bricks.

Laying the bricks

Use a reference string to help align bricks in the pattern you choose for your patio. Begin a herringbone pattern, for example, with a brick set at a 45° angle to the edging in each of two adjacent patio corners. Tap the bricks into the sand with a rubber mallet to make them flush with the edging bricks. Stretch a string between two spare bricks, set just outside the edging, so that the string passes over the corners of the two corner bricks. As you set bricks in the first row, align corners with the string. Use the mallet or adjust the sand bed to keep the bricks even with one another. To begin a new row, lay a brick at each end as a guide for positioning the reference string. Fill in the row, smoothing any sand you may have disturbed. Repeat for each row. Fill triangular spaces along the patio edges with brick that you have cut to fit, then gently sweep sand into any gaps that remain. Add more sand if necessary after it rains.

A CIRCULAR PATIO TO SURROUND A TREE

Edging

Sand

Rubber Mallet

Edging

Half Brick

Starting with half bricks

Loop a garden hose around the tree to mark inner and outer perimeters for the patio. Make the inner circle at least 3 feet in diameter to avoid wide gaps between the half bricks used in the first two courses. Excavate and edge the area to be paved, then prepare the sand bed. Cut half bricks for the first course and tap them into place with a rubber mallet, wedging the inner corners of the bricks tight against each other *(left)*. Use a level to align the tops of the bricks. Trim the last half brick in each course as needed for a snug fit. Lay a second course of half bricks against the first.

Setting the whole bricks

Place concentric circles of whole bricks in the sand bed so that their inner edges touch at the corners and butt against the preceding course. Tap each brick into place with a rubber mallet. Use a 4-foot mason's level to align the brick, adding or removing sand as necessary. Continue laying whole bricks in concentric circles out to the edging.

Filling gaps at the edge

Mark a brick to fit each oddly shaped nook along the patio's outer perimeter. Cut the brick with a brickset as shown on page 120, then trim as needed by chipping it with the sharp end of a mason's hammer. Set the brick into place with a rubber mallet. Gently brush sand into the gaps between bricks, repeating the process as necessary to refill the cracks after a rain.

Brickset

Maul

SETTING BRICKS IN OVERLAPPING SCALLOPS

Scribing scallop arcs

Use the edging of a sand bed to establish a base line for drawing semicircles in the sand. Arcs that have a radius of 24 inches and are spaced with their centers 60 inches apart make an attractive pattern. Scribe arcs across one end of the sand bed, with partial arcs at the sides if necessary. Stretch a string between two bricks so that it crosses the tops of the arcs in the first row *(right)*. Kneeling on boards to avoid disturbing arcs already drawn, scribe another row of arcs with centers midway between those in the first row. A framing square helps in marking these centers and those in subsequent rows. Use partial arcs in the last row if necessary.

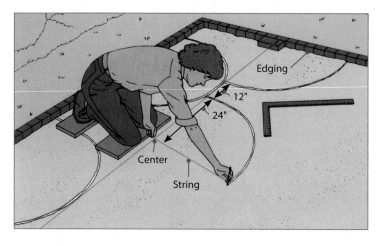

Paving the scallops

Arrange whole bricks along each arc *(left)*, then with a partial brick, start filling each scallop at the narrow space between arcs. Half a brick, followed by three-quarters of a brick in the next course, works well with 24-inch arcs. Pave the rest of each scallop with whole bricks laid in slightly curving rows *(inset)*. Fill partial scallops with whole bricks and any cavities with cut bricks or sand. Sweep sand into any gaps that remain.

Groundwork for a Concrete Slab

A concrete slab consists of a layer of concrete, usually reinforced with wire mesh, that rests on a drainage bed of gravel. Although the 4-inch reinforced slab on 4 inches of gravel described on the following pages satisfies many building codes, always check with local authorities for the correct specifications.

Building codes may also specify the degree of slope required for water runoff and whether a silt fence is needed during construction to limit soil erosion. Local zoning laws may dictate the location, design, and size of a slab.

GETTING STARTED

Selecting a site for a slab requires the same care as choosing one for a brick patio. When your plan is completed use the estimator on page 128 to calculate how much concrete and gravel you'll use, based on the area of the slab and the thickness of the concrete plus the gravel bed.

To prepare the site for a rectangular slab, lay out boundaries with wood stakes and string as shown on page 130, and excavate the site. Dig 2 feet beyond the strings to accommodate form boards and braces, then proceed as shown here. Site preparation for a free-form slab appears on pages 135-137. Save sod and dirt to fill in at the sides of the finished slab.

EXPANSION JOINTS

Many local codes require a strip of asphalt-impregnated expansion-joint filler in the concrete every 8 to 10 feet of a slab's length and between the slab and the house foundation *(page 132)*. The purpose of the joints is to prevent damage as concrete expands and contracts with changes in temperature. Try to buy joint filler as wide as the thickness of the slab. If unavailable, somewhat narrower or wider filler is satisfactory.

FORMS TO SHAPE CONCRETE

Unless you plan on a decorative pattern of permanent form boards *(page 134)*, build forms from inexpensive woods such as fir, spruce, or pine. Plywood, made flexible with the technique shown on page 136, is used to mold the curves of a free-form slab. Double-headed nails allow both types of temporary forms to be quickly disassembled.

SAFETY TIP

Wear goggles when nailing form boards together and joint filler to the house. Gloves protect your hands from blisters, splinters, and especially cuts when handling wire mesh.

TOOLS

- Common carpentry tools
- Spade
- Tamper
- Screed
- Rake
- 4-pound maul
- Line level
- Wire cutters

MATERIALS

- 1-by-2s
- 2-by-4s
- Plywood (¾-inch)
- 2-by-2 stakes
- Mason's cord
- Double-headed nails (2-inch)
- Common nails (3-inch)
- Spikes (6-inch)
- Masonry nails (1½-inch)

- Washed gravel (¾-inch)
- Expansion-joint filler
- Reinforcing mesh
- Binding wire
- Concrete blocks
- Powdered chalk
- Lath

CALCULATIONS FOR SLOPE AND VOLUME

Length of a side boundary line in feet
_____ × 0.25 = _____ inches

Area in square feet	Thickness in inches		
_____ × _____ × 0.0033 = _____ cubic yards			

Calculating slope

For a slope of ¼ inch per foot, use the formula above to determine the difference in height between the edge of the slab that abuts the house and the edge parallel to it. Multiply by 0.125 instead of 0.25 for a slope of ⅛ inch per foot.

Estimating cubic yardage

Use the estimator above to find the amount of concrete or gravel needed for a slab or drainage bed. The result in cubic yards—the bulk measure in which such materials are sold—includes an 8 percent allowance for waste and spillage.

TILTING A SLAB FOR DRAINAGE

Leveling the excavated area

Using a rake, break up any clods of earth; then, with a helper, pull an 8-foot-long 2-by-4 leveling board across the area to smooth it *(above)*. Dampen the area with a hose, and compact the surface by pounding it with a tamper. You can rent one or build one from a 2-foot square of ¾-inch plywood with a braced handle, 4 feet high, made of 2-by-4s. After tamping, pull the leveling board across the area again, using it as a straightedge to make sure that the surface is reasonably even.

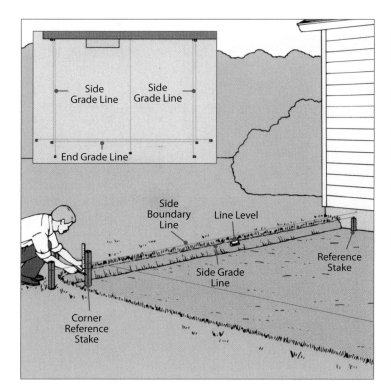

Establishing the grade

Mark the slab height—the sum of the slab and gravel-bed thicknesses—on the house wall, 2 inches outside a side boundary line. Center a 2-by-2 reference stake on the mark and drive it into the ground next to the house wall, bringing the top even with the slab-height mark. Center a nail on top of the stake and hammer it in partway. Measure along the side boundary line to a point 2 inches beyond the end boundary line, and drive a corner reference stake opposite the first. Loop a string around the second stake and tie it to the nail in the other. Hang a line level at the center of the string and adjust the string at the corner stake to make the string level. Use the formula on the preceding page to calculate slope, and mark the resulting distance on the corner stake, below the string. Lower the string to the mark, called a grade mark. Repeat for the other side of the slab. Connect the grade marks on the corner stakes with a third string to make an end grade line. Use that line and a reference stake near the house to establish a grade line within the slab for each expansion joint required.

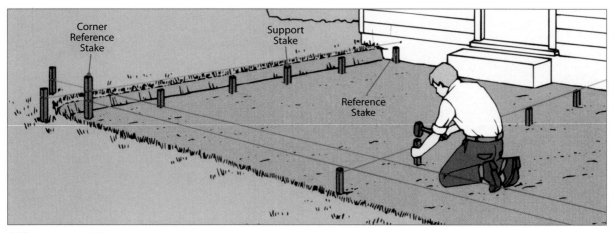

Corner Reference Stake

Support Stake

Reference Stake

Adding support stakes

Mark the grade lines at 2-foot intervals. Directly below each marker, drive a 2-by-2 form-support stake deep enough so you can't pull it out by hand and so the grade line just touches the top of the stake. Place stakes precisely to ensure that corners will be square and the slab sloped correctly. When all of the support stakes are in place, remove the grade lines and use a handsaw to trim the corner reference stakes to the height marked earlier for the grade lines. Then remove all the boundary-marker strings and stakes; leave only the support stakes and the corner reference stakes.

Corner Reference Stake

Installing form boards

Cut a 2-by-4 form board 4 inches longer than the distance from the house to the outer edge of the reference stake. Use more than one if needed, butting the boards. Set a board against the inside faces of the support stakes, one end against the house. Rest the board on wood blocks so that the top edge is even with the tops of the stakes. Drive a 2-inch double-headed nail through each end stake into the board, using a maul as an anvil *(left)*. Then nail the board to the intermediate stakes. Install a form board for the other side of the slab in the same way. Nail a form board for the end of the slab to its support stakes. Where this board abuts the side boards, toenail the joints with 3-inch common nails. For each expansion joint, cut a board ½ inch shorter than the distance between the house and the end board. Nail the board to its support stakes on the side of the slab that will be poured first, leaving a ½-inch space at the wall. Where boards abut *(inset)*, drive a support stake 6 inches to each side of the joint. Nail the boards to the stakes, then nail a strip of ½-inch plywood over the joint.

Bracing the form boards

Drive a support stake at the corners where end and side boards meet. Reinforce each support stake, including those flanking a joint, with a 1-by-2 brace nailed to a stake driven about 1 foot from the form board. Excavate the slab area along the end board to match the slope of the side form boards, then smooth and tamp.

Screeding the gravel

Pour a layer of ¾-inch gravel into each section of the slab, allowing it to spill out under the form boards. With a helper, smooth the gravel by dragging a screed across its surface.

TO MAKE A SCREED

The function of a screed is to assure a smooth gravel surface and a uniform slab thickness. To make the screed shown here, which is designed for a slab 4 inches thick, cut a 1-by-8 board 2 inches shorter than the distance between forms, and a 2-by-4 board 10 inches longer than this distance. Center the 1-by-8 on the 2-by-4. Offset the 1-by-8 board ¼ inch and nail the boards together. To the face of the 1-by-8, toenail two 2-by-2 handles, each 4 feet long and cut at a 30° angle at one end. Brace the handles with 2-by-2s nailed to the top of the 2-by-4.

Installing joint filler

Cut a strip of expansion-joint filler the length of the expansion-joint form. Every foot or so, hammer 3-inch nails through one side of the filler and bend the points slightly to anchor it in the slab. Set the filler against the form (above). Use 6-inch spikes, if necessary, to support the filler at the correct height, even with the top (inset). Nail another strip of filler to the house wall with 1½-inch masonry nails at 6-inch intervals, outlining any existing stairs. Butt the filler against the side form boards and work it into the ½-inch space between expansion-joint forms and the house.

Laying wire mesh

Wearing gloves, unroll mesh over the gravel. Begin at the outer edge of the slab, and leave 2 inches between the mesh and the form boards. Weigh down the mesh with concrete blocks as you go. When you reach the other side of a section, use wirecutters to trim the mesh 2 inches short of the form board. Then turn the mesh over, and walk on it to flatten it. Cover the gravel in the section you intend to pour first, allowing panels of mesh to overlap 6 inches. Cut the mesh to fit around steps or other obstacles, then tie panels together with binding wire.

THE APPEAL OF PERMANENT FORM BOARDS

Expansion Joint

Secondary Board

Primary Board

Perimeter Board

Support Stake

2-By-4 Stake

In most instances, form boards become scrap lumber after a slab is poured. A decorative option, however, is to leave them in place as a frame around the slab or, as shown here, to lay out an attractive pattern of interior form boards. For this purpose, pressure-treated or other weather-resistant wood is superior to the pine or spruce used for temporary forms.

Installing permanent form boards follows the same principles used for setting up temporary boards—with a few differences. When laying out the perimeter for such a slab, take into account that the form boards will contribute to its length and width. Set up and brace perimeter form boards as shown on pages 130-131, but drive support stakes for interior boards as well as perimeter boards an inch below the planned surface of the slab so that the concrete will conceal them.

Establish the slope of the slab as shown on page 129. Each interior board that will lie perpendicular to the house needs a grade line. Boards oriented parallel to the house each require a string set up in the same way as an end line (page 129).

Permanent form boards replace expansion joints within the slab but not the one along the house. Boards that cross from one side of the slab to the other are called primary form boards. Next to the house, use stakes to secure the ends of primary form boards; nail through perimeter form boards to secure other ends.

Secondary form boards are shorter than the width or length of the patio. Where secondary form boards meet perimeter or primary form boards, they can be face-nailed. Where two secondary boards meet, nail one to the other and toenail both to a 2-by-4 stake driven into the ground under the joint.

Before pouring the slab, drive 3-inch nails halfway into all the form boards to help anchor them in the concrete, and cover their top edges with heavy-duty tape to prevent concrete stains.

CURVED FORMS FOR A ROUNDED SLAB

Intermediate Grade Lines

Side Grade Line

End Grade Line

Excavating the slab area

Establish the slab shape with a garden hose, then mark the shape on the ground with powdered chalk. Remove the hose, and excavate the area a distance 2 feet beyond the chalk line. Dig to a depth equal to the thickness of the drainage bed plus the thickness of the slab. Dig back and forth across the area in parallel rows, then smooth and tamp the soil in the bottom of the excavation. Establish drainage away from the house, first by setting up boundary lines and grade lines for a rectangle a foot or two larger in each dimension than the slab's maximum length and width *(inset)*. Tie intermediate grade lines at 3-foot intervals between the side lines, and between the wall of the house and the end line; at the house, tie the strings to masonry nails. Drive 2-by-2 support stakes into the ground around the slab perimeter, 2 feet in from the edge of the excavation. Space the stakes 2 feet apart along gradual curves, 1 foot apart around sharp curves. Add support stakes for any interior forms required, spacing them at 2-foot intervals. Set the tops of the stakes even with the strings.

TAKING THE STIFFNESS OUT OF PLYWOOD

The rigidity of plywood—layers of wood glued together under pressure—results from orienting the grain in each layer perpendicular to the grain in its neighbors. Yet you can make even ¾-inch plywood bend enough to serve as forms for a curved slab. With a circular saw, cut strips about 4 inches wide with the outer grain running lengthwise. Then set the saw for a depth of ½ inch and saw across the strip. Check that the blade cuts through no more than three of the plywood's five layers. Adjust the saw as necessary, then cut grooves across the strip every inch or so.

Plywood   Lath

Installing form boards

To measure for curved form boards, first cut a strip of lath 4 to 8 feet long. Tack it to support stakes, even with the tops and butted against the house. Mark the lath at the midpoint of the support stake nearest the end, then pry off the lath and transfer the mark to a strip of ¾-inch plywood cut as wide as the slab depth. Trim the plywood at the mark. Cut slots in the plywood to make it pliable (*above*), then nail it to the support stakes. Proceed around the slab perimeter in this fashion, butting sections of plywood at support stakes (*inset*). Install expansion-joint forms as necessary (*page 132*).

Sloping the forms

Work around the curved form, lifting or hammering down the boards and stakes until the top edge of the form just grazes the grading lines. Repeat for the straight forms of the expansion joints. When both the curved and the straight forms are adjusted, secure the support stakes with braces *(page 131)*. Correct the depth of the excavation to match the slope of the grade, then spread a gravel drainage bed 4 inches thick. Install joint filler as shown on page 132.

Cutting mesh to fit the form

Unroll a length of wire mesh over a section of the form, letting it overlap the curve of the form boards where necessary. Anchor the mesh temporarily with cinder blocks, then cut the mesh along the curve, 2 inches inside the form. Flatten the mesh either by bending or by removing it from the form and walking it flat. Cut additional sections of mesh, allowing each to overlap the previous section by 6 inches. Flatten the sections and tie them together with binding wire.

Pouring and Finishing Concrete

The key requirement for pouring and finishing a concrete slab is speed. On a dry, windy day, it may take only three hours for freshly poured concrete to become too stiff to work. For a 10-by-12 slab, two people will need about an hour for the heavy work of pouring, leveling, and smoothing the concrete, plus up to three hours to finish the surface. Until you have some experience, it's best to pour concrete in sections no larger than 120 square feet.

MIXING YOUR OWN

A good source of concrete is a ready-mix company specializing in small loads—unless the slab is far from the street. In that case, haul the concrete in a rented trailer and mixer.

When making concrete yourself, test the mixture's consistency frequently *(opposite)*. Between checks, add water sparingly—1 cup per cubic foot of concrete at a time.

PLANNING FOR THE FINISH

Smooth and textured finishes to concrete *(pages 141-142)* need no advance preparation, but surfacing with other materials requires forethought. For example, if you intend to apply a pebble-aggregate surface *(page 143)*, you will need a stiffer-than-average concrete mix. Furthermore, you must thoroughly wet the pebbles before pouring the concrete. Order ⅓ cubic yard of gravel for every 100 square feet of slab.

THE PROCESS OF CURING

After a slab is finished, it must be cured—kept moist and warm for at least a week to allow for the gradual chemical reactions that give concrete its full structural strength. The most common method of curing is to cover the slab with a polyethylene sheet. Colored slabs and pebble-aggregate surfaces are air-cured, however—left uncovered and sprinkled several times a day with water. Wait until the slab has cured to remove the outside forms.

TOOLS

- Concrete mixer
- Shovel
- Rake
- Spade
- 2-by-4 screed
- Bull float
- Ladder
- Mason's trowel
- Edger
- Hand float
- Rectangular trowel
- Convex jointer
- Darby

CONCRETE CHECKLIST

✔ When ordering concrete, tell the ready-mix company the dimensions of your slab and whether you intend to apply a pebble-aggregate surface or wish to have it colored.

✔ If you live in an area subject to freezes and thaws, make sure that an air-entraining agent—a chemical that creates tiny air bubbles in the concrete to prevent cracking—is added to the mix.

✔ Make arrangements for the ready-mix truck to arrive early; concrete sets more slowly in the cool of the morning.

✔ Have the truck park on the street, then lay a path of planks for carrying the concrete to the slab in wheelbarrows.

✔ Transport approximately 1 cubic foot (150 pounds) in a wheelbarrow at a time.

PERFECT CONCRETE

Mixing the correct amount of water into concrete is crucial: Too little and a smooth finish on the concrete will be difficult to attain, too much and the material will lack strength and durability. The concrete in the near photograph, although appearing somewhat dry, is actually just right; light troweling produces a smooth surface. A dash or two more water produces a mudlike mixture that is too wet for use *(far)*.

FILLING THE FORMS

Adding the concrete

Support the wire mesh on bricks, and oil the form boards to prevent sticking. Dump enough concrete into the first form to overfill by ½ inch a 3- to 4-foot-wide section between the form boards, packing each load against the preceding one with a shovel. Use the shovel after each load to push the concrete into form corners and against the joint filler. Work a flat spade between the forms and the concrete to force the stones in the mix away from the sides. Then jab the spade vertically into the concrete throughout the section, to eliminate air pockets. If the wire reinforcement sags into the gravel base under the concrete's weight, hook it with a rake and lift it to the middle of the concrete.

Screeding the concrete

As each 3- to 4-foot section is filled, set a screed—a straight 2-by-4, cut 2 feet wider than the width of the form—on edge across the form boards. With the aid of a helper, lift and lower the screed in a chopping motion to force the aggregate down into the concrete. Then, starting at one end of the filled section, pull the screed across the surface of the concrete, simultaneously sliding it from side to side in a sawlike motion. Tilt the screed toward you as you pull it, so that the bottom of the board acts as a cutting edge. To level any remaining low spots or bumps, pull the screed across the concrete again, tilting it away from you. In areas around obstacles such as steps or window wells, use a short screed, cut to fit the space. Fill and level the rest of the form in successive 3- to 4-foot sections.

Bull-floating the surface

To compact and smooth the concrete, first push the float forward, tilting the front edge of the blade upward. Then draw it back, keeping the blade flat against the surface. Shovel fresh concrete into any remaining depressions. To reach areas beyond arm's length, bridge the wet concrete with a ladder supported on concrete blocks. Bull-float the surface again.

Edging the concrete

When the concrete is firm enough to hold its shape, run a mason's trowel between the form boards and the outside edge of the slab to separate the top inch of concrete from the wood *(above, right)*. Push an edger back and forth along the slot *(above, left)*, tilting the leading edge of the tool slightly upward to avoid gouging the concrete. Any deep indentations will be difficult to fill during later finishing steps. Wait for any surface water to evaporate from the slab before applying the finish.

FINISHING THE SURFACE

Trowel

Float

Troweling a smooth finish

Place a pair of knee boards—1- by 2-foot pieces of ⅜-inch plywood with 2-by-2 handles nailed at the ends—on the slab. Kneeling on the boards, smooth the concrete with a hand float, holding it flat and sweeping it in overlapping arcs across the surface. Then sweep a rectangular steel trowel, held flat, across the same area. Similarly float and trowel the rest of the slab, moving the knee boards as necessary. *(The concrete will be firm enough to walk on at this stage.)* After floating and troweling, go over the slab again with the trowel alone, this time tilting the tool slightly. Work the surface until no concrete collects on the trowel and the blade makes a ringing sound indicating that the concrete is too firm to work any further. Run the edger between the form boards and the edges of the slab *(above)* to restore edging lines.

Brooming a skidproof surface

Hand-float the concrete and trowel it once (*page 141*). Instead of the final troweling, draw a damp, stiff-bristled utility brush across the surface. Either score straight lines at right angles to the forms or move the broom in arcs to produce a curved pattern. If the broom picks up small lumps of concrete, hose down the bristles to clean them; give the slab a few more minutes' drying time before you continue. If you have to press hard to score the concrete, work fast; the concrete will soon be too firm to take a finish.

Convex Jointer

Creating a flagstone effect

Immediately after bull-floating the concrete (*page 140*), score the surface with irregularly spaced grooves, ½- to ¾-inch deep, using a convex jointer. Place a ladder across the forms as a bridge to reach inaccessible spots. After surface water has evaporated, hand-float and trowel the surface, then retool the grooves to restore the flagstone pattern to its original clarity. Brush out the grooves with a dry paintbrush to remove any remaining loose bits of concrete.

PEBBLES FOR A TOPCOAT

Preparing the surface

Fill the form with concrete as on page 140, but pack it even with the tops of the boards rather than above them. Level the concrete with a screed notched at each end so that its bottom edge rides ½ inch below the tops of the form boards, then bull-float the surface. Scatter the damp pebbles evenly over the concrete with a shovel. Cover the surface with a single layer of stones, using a ladder bridge, if necessary, to reach inner areas.

Embedding the aggregate

Tap the stones into the concrete with a bull float, forcing them just below the surface. After you have gone over the entire slab with the bull float, press down any stones that are still visible with a hand float, using a ladder bridge, if needed, to reach the interior of the slab. Then run the hand float across the surface as on page 141, covering the stones with a thin, smooth layer of concrete.

Exposing the aggregate

After surface water has evaporated and the concrete is firm enough to resist indentation, brush the surface lightly with a stiff nylon broom to expose the tops of the stones. While a helper sprays the slab with water, brush it again, uncovering between a quarter and a half of the stones' circumference. If you dislodge any stones, stop brushing and wait until the concrete is a bit firmer before continuing. If the concrete is difficult to wash off, work quickly to expose the aggregate before the surface becomes too stiff. After exposing the stones, continue to spray the surface until there is no noticeable cement film left on the aggregate. Scrub individual spots missed in the general wash with a scrub brush and a pail of water. Two to four hours after exposing the aggregate, wash and lightly brush the surface again to remove any cloudy residue from the stones.

A Curved Bench beside a Free-Form Patio

A wood bench is a handsome addendum to any patio. The design shown here—for a bench shaped to a curved patio—is easily adapted to a rectangular one.

Choose a wood that is sufficiently resistant to decay and insects to be used outdoors. Cedar, cypress, and redwood stand up well.

Anchoring posts

Use a 3-foot length of lath as a guide for chalking posthole marks on the edge of the patio *(left)*. Dig a hole about 7 inches wide, 11 inches long, and 1 foot deep centered on each mark. Cut a 3-foot-long 4-by-4 post for each hole, and anchor the posts in concrete. Let the concrete set for 48 hours. Mark each post 15½ inches above ground level and trim to that height.

Installing crosspieces

Cut two 3½-inch by 1-inch notches in the top of each post. For each notch, cut a 2-by-4 crosspiece, 17¾ inches long. Center the crosspieces in the notches and nail them in place with 2½-inch galvanized nails. Drill two ⅜-inch holes, diagonally spaced, through the braces and posts. Fasten the crosspieces with 5-inch galvanized carriage bolts—or use brass ones from a marine-supply store.

Making the seat

Cut fifteen 1-by-2 slats long enough—at least 7 feet—to overhang the end-most crosspieces. Rip several ⅜-inch strips from a 2-by-4, and cut them into 5-inch spacers, 42 in all. Position a slat so that it extends beyond the ends of the crosspieces by about ¼ inch *(left)*, and nail it, edge up, to the crosspieces with 3-inch galvanized finishing nails, beginning at the center post. Next, set a spacer on each post, next to the slat. Alternate the slats with spacers to cover the crosspieces. Then, saw off the ends of the slats parallel to the end crosspieces. Add 1-by-2 caps to the ends of the slats *(inset)*. Fasten with 2-inch brass or galvanized wood screws. Reinforce outside slats with a screw driven through them into the spacers behind them.

Spacer

Cap

Brick or Flagstone Set in Mortar

Brick or flagstone set in mortar can transform a drab concrete slab into an attractive focus for relaxing and entertaining. Unless you have recently poured a new slab, test it for soundness before proceeding. Regardless of results—and no matter how new the concrete—use a metal straightedge to check the entire surface for high and low spots. Bricks and flagstones may rock on high spots and break loose. Water can collect in low spots and cause mortar to deteriorate.

Flatten high spots with a mason's rubbing brick or with a silicon carbide wheel in an electric drill. Break up low spots covering more than 1 square foot with a cold chisel and fill them as you would a hole.

ESTIMATING MATERIALS

Find the area of the slab. *(For a free-form slab, use the method shown on page 122.)* You will need 4½ paving bricks to 1 square foot. For materials with nonstandard dimensions and for flagstones, consult a dealer. In either case, add about 5 percent for breakage and repair. Some flagstones are soft enough to be cut with a brickset; others are so hard that they must be scored with a masonry blade in a circular saw.

One cubic foot of mortar mix is enough to lay about 35 bricks or 12 square feet of flagstones. Buy additional mix to grout joints between bricks and flagstones.

LAYING A DRY RUN

Arranging the bricks or stones in a dry run is an essential first step. With bricks, orient the long sides with the slope of the slab. Doing so channels rainwater away from the house. Use a piece of ½-inch plywood to space a row of bricks along two adjacent sides of the slab, trimming bricks as needed *(page 120)* to fill the rows. Leave the dry run in place as a guide for a string marker.

In a dry run of flagstones, vary the sizes of adjacent stones to avoid long joint lines. Spaces between stones should range from ½ inch to 2 inches wide. Large gaps can be filled with pieces cut from stones that overlap.

EXPANSION JOINTS

Always leave the expansion joint between the slab and the house uncovered. At the end of the job, after the mortar has set, press polyethylene rope into the joint, then cover the rope with self-leveling polysulfide or silicone caulk. If the slab is divided by expansion joints, matching joints are required when veneering with brick but not with flagstones, which can withstand expansion forces that can crack or loosen brick.

A FRAME AROUND THE PATIO

You may want to install edging around brick or flagstone to protect vulnerable corners and cover the sides of the patio. Set pressure-treated 2-by-8s or 2-by-10s in the ground on edge, even with the veneer surface. Metal edging is available for free-form slabs. An application of masonry sealant helps prevent the growth of moss and mildew, which can be unsightly and slippery.

MORTAR AND GROUT

✔ Buy type M mortar, available premixed from building suppliers.

✔ Mix batches no larger than you can use in 10 to 15 minutes, about half a bag.

✔ Heap the dry ingredients in a wheelbarrow or mortar tub and make a depression in the center. Into the depression, gradually pour cold water as recommended by the manufacturer. Stir with a hoe.

✔ Mortar should be just wet enough to slide easily off the hoe. Grout should have the consistency of a thick milkshake. Both must be completely free of lumps.

✔ Before mixing a new batch, scrape or rinse all dried mortar out of the mortar tub.

✔ Moisten both the slab and the veneering materials before beginning work so they will not absorb water from your mortar and grout.

TOOLS

- Mason's rubbing brick
- 2-by-2 stakes
- Mason's cord
- Cold chisel
- Brickset
- Mason's hammer
- 4-pound maul
- Rubber mallet
- Mortar tub
- Hoe
- Mason's trowel
- Pointing trowel
- ½-inch joint filler
- Grout bag
- Wire brush

MATERIALS

- Bricks or flagstones
- Mortar mix
- Chalk
- Muriatic acid
- Masonry sealant

BRICK VENEER FOR A CONCRETE SLAB

Setting brick in mortar

Use a large mason's trowel to spread a ½-inch layer of mortar on the rough face of the first brick in the dry run. Make a shallow groove in the mortar with the point of the trowel. Set the brick at the edge of the slab and tamp it firmly with the trowel handle to level it. Working one brick at a time, use the ½-inch plywood spacer to position succeeding bricks. Level the bricks before proceeding. Stake a guide string to align bricks of the second course with the second brick of the dry run. Where a house wall prevents the use of a stake, tie the string to a brick and set it on a scrap of ½-inch plywood. Level the bricks in each course, then reposition the guide string for the next Wait at least 24 hours before proceeding to the next step.

Grouting the joints

Fill a grout bag with a ½-inch nozzle about two-thirds full and roll the top to squeeze grout into the gaps between bricks. With a ½-inch joint filler, pack the grout into the gaps to a level slightly below the brick surfaces to make a drainage channel. Smooth the grout with the joint filler. Wait an hour, then remove ragged bits of grout with the trowel. Three hours later, smooth the joints with a wire brush, and hose the patio clean. Allow the grout to cure for several days. Then remove any grout stains on the bricks with a mild solution of muriatic acid and a wire brush. Hose away the residue.

> ## SAFETY TIP
>
> Use leather-palmed gloves to protect your hands from rough edges of brick or stone. Irritants in mortar and grout call for a dust mask and gloves. Wear goggles when grinding or chipping at a slab, mixing mortar, cutting brick or stone, or when working with muriatic acid.

RANDOM SHAPES FROM FLAGSTONES

Laying out a dry run

Arrange the flagstones on the slab allowing ½- to 2-inch gaps between adjacent stones. Ignore any expansion joints except the one adjacent to the house wall. Where a stone hangs over the edge of the slab, mark a cutting line on it with chalk, using the edge of the slab as a guide. Where stones overlap each other, mark one of the stones, allowing space for the mortar joint between them. Cutting lines should be straight; you can approximate a curve with several short cuts.

Cutting a stone

Remove marked stones one by one and score each for cutting. To do so, hold a brick-set against the chalk line and tap it several times with a maul *(above, left)*; then move the brickset along the line and tap again. For stones that are more than 1 inch thick, score a corresponding line on the other side by extending the first line down the edges of the stone and marking a connecting line on the back. Rest the stone on a board, with the scored line no more than ¼ inch beyond the edge. Then tap the overhang with the maul to snap it off *(above, right)*. As each stone is cut, return it to its position on the slab.

Laying the stones in mortar

At a corner or along an edge, set a section of stones about 4 by 4 feet in area next to the slab as they were arranged in the dry run. Moisten the exposed slab with water, then trowel on a 1-inch-thick mortar bed. Position the stones on the mortar, seating them with a rubber mallet. Fill any large spaces with pieces of cut stone.

Making an even surface

Examine the flagstones just laid. If a stone sits too high, lift it aside and scoop out some of the mortar with a pointing trowel. If a stone is too low, add mortar and smooth it with the trowel to ensure a good bond. Finish each section by using a pointing trowel or a tongue depressor to remove any excess mortar that has pushed up between stones. Sponge stray mortar off the stones.

Grouting the joints

After the mortar has cured 24 to 48 hours, trowel grout into the joints. Then use a joint filler to compact the grout to a depth of $\frac{1}{16}$ inch below the stone surface. Wipe away excess grout with a wet rag within 10 minutes to prevent stains. Do not use muriatic acid; it may discolor flagstone. To ensure that the wide joints between flagstones cure adequately, mist the stonework with water every four hours for the first day, and allow the grout to cure three more days before walking on the patio.

The Many Possibilities of Tile

Hard-fired ceramic-clay tiles set in mortar on a concrete slab offer attractive, durable choices for outdoor patios or at poolside. Any outdoor tile must be frost-proof; purchase tile with an absorption rate of 6 percent or less.

TYPES OF TILE

Quarry tiles have a smooth surface and come in squares, rectangles, hexagons, and octagons of various sizes. Paver tiles are thicker than quarry tiles and are commonly cast in squares and hexagons with a textured surface and rough or rounded edges.

Mosaic tiles, mounted for correct spacing on a 1- or 2-foot-square mesh backing, make fast work of intricate designs. For outdoor use, choose mosaic tiles with a matte glaze so the surface will not be slippery when it is wet.

PRELIMINARY STEPS

First, check the slab you intend to tile for flaws. To estimate the number of tiles you need, calculate the area of the slab *(page 122)*, and purchase tile accordingly.

LAYING A DRY RUN

Note the position of expansion joints, if any, between sections of slab, and design your tile pattern around them *(page 155)*. Lay a dry run of tile to ensure accurate placement. Plastic spacers or lugs molded into the edges of tiles help position them precisely.

CUTTING TILES

You can cut quarry tiles with the hand tools shown on pages 156 and 157. Buy the micro-cutter and nippers; rent the more expensive senior cutter.

Tiles more than ½-inch thick require a circular saw with a silicon carbide masonry blade or an electric tub saw, in which water cools the blade and flushes away ceramic chips and dust. Regardless of the tool you use, always cut ribbed tiles across the ribs.

LATEX-BASE MORTAR

A tiled patio lasts longer and requires less maintenance when the mortar for anchoring the tiles and the grout for filling joints between them are made with a latex tile-setting liquid instead of water. Ceramic-tile grout comes premixed in a variety of colors; a 10-pound bag is enough for about 10 square feet of paver or quarry tile, or 20 square feet of mosaic tile. You can make your own grout by mixing equal parts of Portland cement and fine masonry sand with enough latex liquid to make a thick paste.

When you are ready to lay tiles, dampen the slab and trowel on a thin bed of mortar. Set the tiles in small sections while the mortar is still soft, planning the work so that you do not disturb freshly laid tiles.

Allow the mortar to cure 24 hours before grouting the joints. Do the grouting within the next 24 hours, however, to ensure a solid bond to the mortar.

PRESERVING YOUR PATIO

To protect tiles and grout from stains, you can seal the finished paving with commercial masonry sealer or a 5 percent silicone solution. You may prefer to seal only the grout, which usually is lighter and more absorbent than the tile and shows stains more readily.

TOOLS

- Tile cutters
- Mortar tub
- Mason's trowel
- Notched trowel
- Grout float
- Caulking gun

MATERIALS

- Tile spacers
- Mortar/grout mix
- Latex tile-setting liquid
- Polyethylene-foam rope
- Silicone or polysulfide caulk
- Masonry sealer

SAFETY TIP

When cutting tile, wear safety goggles and heavy work gloves to protect yourself against chips and sharp edges.

A typical tile

Outdoor tiles like the textured example above commonly have ribbed backs to improve the bond between mortar and tile. Most tiles are available in a bullnose shape, rounded on one edge or two and used along the perimeter and at the corners of a patio.

A variety of shapes and colors

The square tile above, perhaps the most familiar, is just one of many styles available. Six-sided tiles are best used alone, but 8-sided tiles can be combined with small squares in an octagon-and-dot pattern *(opposite, middle row, left)*. Besides traditional terra cotta, tiles come in many colors and patterns, including a wood-grain finish *(above)*.

COMPOSING PATTERNS WITH SHAPED TILES

Repeating a single shape

Some patterns are inherent in the shapes of tiles. At far left is a stacked pattern of rectangular tiles—square ones are also suitable. At left is a honeycomb formed of hexagons; octagons may also be used.

Repeating two shapes

The octagon-and-dot pattern *(right)* builds automatically with 8-inch octagons and 3-inch squares, or dots. A square-and-picket pattern *(far right)* builds from 8-inch squares surrounded by 3-by 11-inch pickets.

Patterns from many shapes

Rectangular and square tiles, whose dimensions are multiples of the smallest unit, make a lively pattern with little cutting *(near)*. The rubble pattern is achieved using broken paver tiles with their edges smoothed.

STARTING THE TILE SEQUENCE

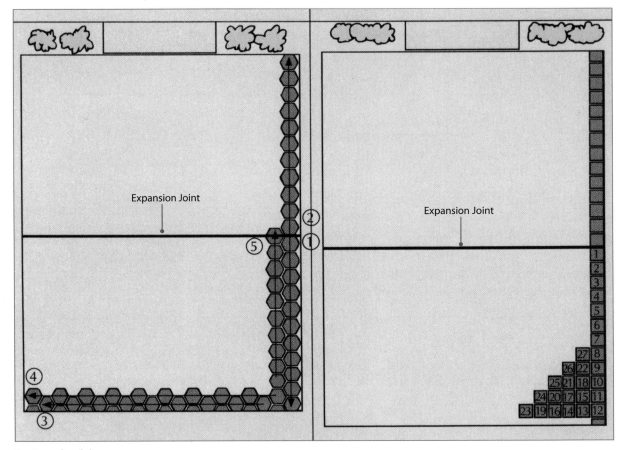

Rectangular slabs

If there is an expansion joint, begin work there. For 6- or 8-sided tiles, set the first row to a far corner *(above left, Arrow 1)*, trimming a tile at the end of the row if necessary. Extend the row toward the house *(Arrow 2)*, leaving a gap at the joint; trim the corner tile as needed. Using the last full tile nearest the far corner as a guide, set a row of tiles perpendicular to the first, along the edge of the slab *(Arrow 3)*. Alternate tiles may have to be cut. Set succeeding rows *(Arrows 4 and 5)* in the same manner, letting some tiles bridge the expansion joint, until the entire slab is covered. Finally, cut tiles to fill in the gaps remaining around the edge. For square or rectangular tiles in a simple stack pattern, follow the numbers *(above, right)* to set the first row out to a far corner. There, use the last full tile as the apex of a triangle, and set tiles in diagonal rows until one section of the slab is covered, then proceed with the other section. Cut tiles to fill any gaps left around the edges.

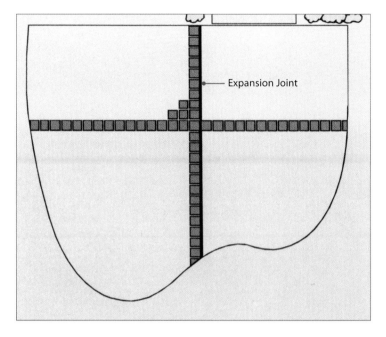

Expansion Joint

Free-form slabs

If the shape of the slab is irregular or curved, snap perpendicular chalk lines across its widest dimensions or use expansion joints to divide it into quadrants. Starting at the intersection near the center of the patio, lay tile along each axis toward the edges. Mark tiles for cutting as necessary. Then fill in each quadrant as shown left.

Interrupted slabs

To tile around a tree or pool, first lay a rectangular frame around the obstacle, then fill in the frame as necessary with tiles trimmed to fit. Add an edge of border tiles, if desired. Divide the slab into quadrants, using a tile at the midpoint of each side of the frame as a reference point. Lay rows of tiles along the quadrant lines, and fill in each section with parallel rows of tiles. Cut the outermost tile in each row to fit the edge of the slab.

Frame

THREE TECHNIQUES FOR CUTTING TILES

Using a senior cutter

Place a marked tile on the cutter plate, with the cutting line directly above the breaking bar. Set and lock the adjustable fence to hold the tile firmly in place. Slide the cutter handle toward you, then lift the handle until the scoring wheel rests on the line. Push the handle forward in one continuous motion, scoring the tile. Rest the flanges on the tile at its midpoint, then strike the handle sharply with your fist *(right)*, causing the flanges to snap the tile over the breaking bar.

Using a microcutter

On the tile, draw a cutting line; it may be straight or gently curved. Set the scoring wheel on the line, hold the tile firm, and run the scoring wheel along the line in one continuous motion. For a straight cut, use a plywood scrap or uncut tile as a guide. Follow curves freehand. In either case, score the tile once; a second pass increases the chance of a ragged break. Center the jaws of the cutter on the scored line *(above)* and squeeze the cutter handles. The tile will snap along the scored line.

Cutting with tile nippers
Score a cutting line on the tile followed by a crosshatch pattern in the area to be cut away. Grasping the tile firmly in one hand, work from the edge toward the cutting line, chipping off small pieces. Hold the nippers with the jaws at an angle to the section of line you are approaching. When the rough cut is complete, smooth the edges with a piece of brick or a small stone.

LAYING TILES ON MORTAR

Applying the mortar bed
Set dry-run tiles next to the slab, then spray the concrete with water in the area to be tiled first. Working in sections of 3 square feet or so, spread a thin layer of mortar over the dampened slab with the smooth edge of a rectangular notched-blade trowel. Turn the trowel and draw the notched edge through the mortar, leaving a pattern of uniform ridges. Keep a pointing trowel nearby for removing excess mortar and scraping dripped mortar from the slab. Rinse both trowels often in a bucket of water, to remove mortar before it dries.

Laying the tiles

Hold a tile by its edges and lower it onto the mortar bed with as little sideways motion as possible. Tap the tile with a rubber mallet to seat it firmly. Unless your tiles are molded with spacer lugs, lay plastic spacers on the mortar at the corners of the tile, then place the second tile against the spacers. Lay all the full tiles, checking the tiled surface every 4 or 5 tiles for evenness. When laying interlocking tiles near an expansion joint, stand ⅜-inch furniture dowels—available in bulk at hardware stores or home-improvement centers—between the tiles next to the joint *(inset)*. Cut tiles for the edge of the slab as needed and mortar them in place. Allow the mortar to cure for 24 hours.

Spacer

Expansion Joint

Dowel

FILLING JOINTS WITH GROUT

Grouting the joints

If you used plastic spacers between tiles—and they are less than ¼ inch below the tiled surface—remove them. Extract any dowel spacers near an expansion joint and gently fill the gap with strips of rolled newspaper to keep it free of grout. Place small mounds of grout at intervals along the mortar joints over an area 3- or 4-feet square. Kneeling on a piece of plywood to distribute your weight and avoid dislodging tiles, force the grout between the tiles with a rubber grout float dampened with water. Dip the float in a bucket of water occasionally to keep it wet.

Cleaning the tiles

Let the grout dry for about 10 minutes, but not longer than specified by the manufacturer. Wipe away any excess grout with a damp sponge, using a light, circular motion. Rinse the sponge often in clean water, but wring it well to avoid saturating the grout or washing the pigment out of colored grout. Mist the tiled surface with water every 4 hours for the first day, to let the grout cure slowly. After the third day, remove hazy grout residue from the tile surface by buffing with a dry cloth.

Filling the expansion joint

After the grout has cured, remove the rolled newspaper from the expansion joint and press ⅜-inch polyethylene-foam rope to the bottom of the gap *(above, left)*. Fill any space remaining with silicone or poly-sulfide caulk *(above, right)*, wiping excess caulk off the tiles immediately with the solvent recommended by the manufacturer. Let the caulk dry before walking on the tiles. If you intend to seal the tiles, wait a week or more to allow the grout to dry completely, then apply two coats of sealer.

CHAPTER 5

Fences and Walls

Before putting up a structure in the outdoors, there is a certain amount of groundwork to do. The first step often involves defining the limits of your property. This could be as simple as finding your property markers. Or you may have to master the rudiments of operating a transit level—a relatively straightforward task. If your land is sloping or uneven you also may need to terrace the area to create a level spot for your building.

There are many reasons to raise a fence or build a wall, from increasing privacy to discouraging trespassers. The effect can be as imposing as a solid brick wall or as neighborly as that symbol of a quiet suburban home—the picket fence. But no matter what type of structure you decide to erect, there are certain fundamentals that need to be mastered to ensure that it will be both attractive and long-lasting.

The white picket fence is
a time-honored classic.

Both of these designs use stone walls to striking effect.

The stone wall and flowers soften the visual impact of this high wooden fence.

An elegant fence or wall can provide privacy and security without detracting visually from your landscaping plan.

Basic Surveying Techniques

Before building any outdoor structure near a neighbor's land, be sure you know exactly where your property lines lie. Start by studying the lot plat, or map, that was furnished with the title to the land. When mapping the land, the surveyors drove metal stakes into the ground at the corners of the plot to serve as property markers. If you can locate one of them, your property map and a little basic geometry will enable you to find the others. You can determine the boundaries by driving stakes next to the markers, then stretching string between the stakes.

Once the boundaries are established, a few simple surveying techniques and tools will enable you to map the location and size of the structure you want to build. Distances can be measured fairly accurately with a mason's line, wooden stakes, and a carpenter's tape measure, but keep at least 12 inches from a property line when siting a structure to avoid accidentally straying onto a neighbor's land. To sight lines for pouring foundations, or to establish perfect parallels or right angles to property lines, use a transit level.

TOOLS	MATERIALS
■ Tape measure	■ Wooden stakes
■ Maul	■ Tall poles
■ Shovel	■ Powdered chalk
■ Magnetic stud finder	■ Mason's line
■ Transit level	■ Clear plastic hose

CAUTION

Before positioning or excavating trenches, find the locations of underground obstacles such as dry wells, septic tanks, and cesspools, and electric, water, and sewer lines.

FINDING PROPERTY MARKERS

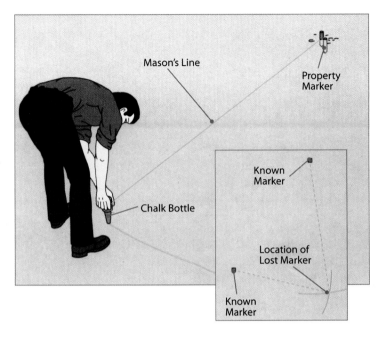

Working from two known markers
With a maul, drive a wooden stake next to a known marker. (Property markers may be lost in undergrowth or a few inches underground.) Attach a length of mason's line equal to the distance between the known marker and the lost marker, as indicated on your property map. Mark an arc on the ground near the lost marker with powdered chalk *(left)*. Repeat the procedure at another known marker. Dig for the lost marker at the intersection of the arcs *(inset)*.

Working from a single marker
Mark an arc on the ground with chalk over the approximate location of the hidden marker *(above)*. Brush a magnetic stud finder along the arc *(right)*. When the stud finder's needle deflects, dig for the marker. If the stud finder does not work, try using a metal detector. The final recourse is to call in a professional surveyor to reestablish the property lines.

SIMPLE SIGHTING AND LEVELING TECHNIQUES

Sighting a straight line over a hill

Drive a stake at both the starting and unseen points. Stand at one stake, station a helper at the other, and have two more helpers hold tall poles in between at points where the tops of the poles can be seen from both stake positions *(right and inset)*. Sighting from your stake, signal the pole holder nearest you to move until the two poles are in a straight line from your view. Have the helper at the unseen point repeat the procedure with the second pole person. Alternate sightings until the poles appear in line from both positions. Connect the four points with mason's line.

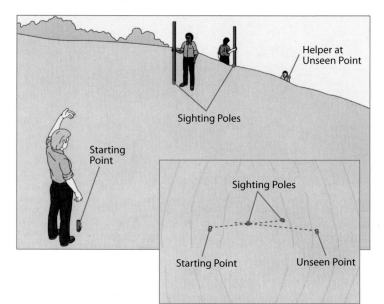

Finding level points on a slope

You can find a point on a stake or post that is level with a mark on another by using a water level or a clear plastic hose partly filled with water. Make a mark at the desired or known height on the first post. Position the hose between the posts as shown. Hold one end a few inches above the mark you have made and have a helper hold the other end at about the same height. Fill the hose with water until the level reaches the mark. Make sure there are no air bubbles—if there are, block and lower one end to allow the bubble to rise to the surface. Finally, mark the second post at the water level in the hose *(left)*.

A TELESCOPE THAT MEASURES ANGLES

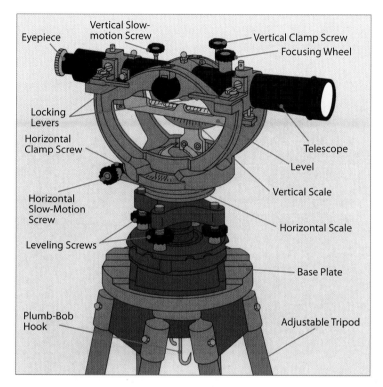

Eyepiece

Vertical Slow-motion Screw

Vertical Clamp Screw

Focusing Wheel

Locking Levers

Horizontal Clamp Screw

Telescope

Level

Horizontal Slow-Motion Screw

Vertical Scale

Leveling Screws

Horizontal Scale

Base Plate

Plumb-Bob Hook

Adjustable Tripod

Anatomy of a transit level

This professional surveying tool is essentially a tripod-mounted movable telescope with precise scales for reading vertical and horizontal angles. The 20-power telescope pivots at its center for vertical measurements and the entire mounting carriage rotates on the undercarriage for horizontal ones. A small spirit level mounted under the telescope assists in leveling and plumbing the instrument. A hook for a plumb bob hangs from the base plate; the undercarriage slides over the base plate to position the bob over a stake or marker, and four leveling screws are used to set the level. Angles are measured on vertical and horizontal scales; when only horizontal measurements are needed, as on the following pages, a pair of levers locks the telescope in the level position. Slow-motion screws allow you to zero in on the sighting stake by turning the telescope; clamp screws then lock the transit in position.

DIFFERENT SCALES FOR DIFFERENT ANGLES

In addition to setting straight lines or right angles *(page 166)*, a transit level can be used to measure a range of horizontal and vertical angles. Horizontal angles are read on a 360-degree circular scale divided into four 90-degree arcs *(top left)*, vertical angles on a 90-degree arc *(bottom)*. Small auxiliary scales called verniers serve as pointers for the main scales and give readings in sixtieths of a degree, or minutes.

If the zero mark on the vernier falls between two degree marks on the main scale, read the lower mark and use the vernier to calculate the fraction in minutes. Reading upward from the degree mark, find the mark on the vernier that lines up perfectly with a mark on the main scale. Count the vernier spaces between the two main-scale marks. Each space stands for 5 minutes; multiply the number of spaces by five to get a reading in minutes. The sighting at right reads 17 degrees 15 minutes.

Horizontal Scale

Vernier

17 Degrees 15 Minutes

Vernier

Vertical Scale

Vernier

SETTING UP A TRANSIT LEVEL

Positioning the tripod

Spread the tripod legs over a marker to be used as a starting point. Move the legs one at a time until the plumb bob hangs no more than ¼ inch from the center of the marker. Loosen the screw under the base plate and shift the transit level so the plumb bob is directly over the center of the stake. Tighten the base-plate screw.

Base-Plate Screw

Plumb Bob

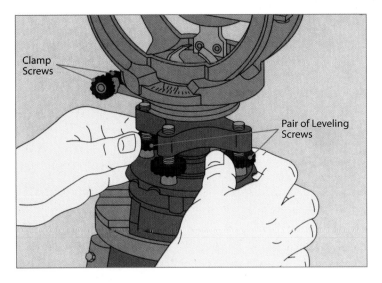

Clamp Screws

Pair of Leveling Screws

Leveling the transit

Set the vertical scale to zero. Loosen the horizontal clamp screws and turn the telescope until it aligns with one pair of leveling screws. Turn these screws until the bubble in the level is centered *(left)*. Rotate the telescope 90 degrees to align it with the other pair of screws; adjust these screws the same way. Repeat as needed, making minor adjustments so the bubble in the level remains centered as the telescope swings full circle.

A LASER TRANSIT

The laser transit replaces the telescope of a traditional transit by emitting a laser beam, which enables the device to be used by one person. A traditional transit requires two people—one at the telescope and another at the target. But the laser transit can be aimed by the user who can then go to the target and observe the beam.

PRECISE LINES AND ANGLES

A line over a long distance
Drive stakes at the two points to be aligned and prepare an intermediate sighting pole for each of the major peaks and valleys between the stakes. Position and level the transit over the starting stake as shown on page 168. Focus on the far pole and tighten the horizontal clamp screw. Have a helper hold the furthest intermediate stake at its approximate position *(right)*, moving it until it is centered in your field of vision, then drive the stake into the ground. Repeat the procedure for the other stakes.

Sighting Pole

Setting a right angle

Set a straight line to a stake, as shown here. Rotate the transit level exactly 90 degrees on the horizontal scale and tighten the horizontal clamp screw to lock it in position. Have a helper move another pole until you sight it in the cross hairs *(right)*, then drive the pole in place. Check the angle by swinging the transit level back 90 degrees to the original pole and ensuring it is sighted in the cross hairs.

SIGHTING A PARALLEL LINE AROUND AN OBSTRUCTION

Point B

Point D

Point A

Point C (Starting Point)

Plotting an approximate parallel

You may need to set a line parallel to one that is obstructed, such as property line A-B in this example. Set up the transit over a starting stake where the view is unobstructed and sight a line roughly parallel to line A-B *(above)*. On this line, drive a stake at point D so that lines A-B and C-D are equal in length. Stretch a mason's line between points C and D.

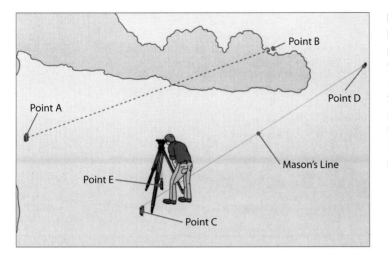

Locating the first stake

From point C, rotate the transit 90 degrees toward point A. Move the transit along the mason's line so that the cross hairs align with the stake at point A *(left)*. Rotate the transit 90 degrees toward point D to line up the cross hairs with the stake; adjust the position of the transit as necessary, so that it rests at the apex of a 90-degree angle between points A and D. Drive a stake directly underneath the transit—at point E.

Locating the second stake

Measure the distance between points A and E, and cut a length of the mason's line equal to that distance. Attach the line to the stake at point B and swing it toward point D, making an arc. Loosen the line joining points C and D, fasten one end to the stake at point E, and swing the other end in an arc toward point D. Plant a stake where the two arcs intersect (point F). The line joining points E and F is now parallel to the property line between points A and B.

Creating Terraced Landings

The land surrounding your home may be hilly, making it difficult to find a level spot to erect a structure. Often the solution is to create a terrace by building a retaining wall.

Earth and water exert considerable pressure behind a retaining wall, so you must make your structure strong and provide adequate drainage. Begin by checking your local regulations on drainage (any change in the contour of your land will affect the flow of water) and any other restrictions.

MODULAR "STONE" WALL

Special concrete wall blocks *(page 174)* create the look of a stone wall in a fraction of the time and are just as strong. Depending on their design, they can be raised to a height of 24 to 48 inches without any anchoring. Each row of blocks is linked to the one above with matching grooves and ledges. The front face of the blocks is usually wider than the back, making it easy to create circular and serpentine walls.

A PALISADE OF POSTS

For a simple retaining wall up to 36 inches high, plant a row of vertical timbers in the ground and spike the timbers together with bars of reinforcing steel. "Found" materials such as old pier pilings or telephone poles make strong and economical choices for building supplies.

LIMITATIONS

The terraces created by these walls are suitable for light-duty demands. Walls supporting terraces for heavier loads, especially dynamic loads like vehicular traffic, need extra anchoring and should be referred to a structural engineer. Also, walls higher than 36 inches often require a building permit and are best left to a professional.

TOOLS	MATERIALS
■ Tape measure	■ Stakes
■ Carpenter's level	■ Posts
■ Line level	■ Reinforcing bar (⅜")
■ Rake	■ Coarse sand
■ Shovel	■ ¾ drainage aggregate
■ Square-edged spade	■ Gravel
■ Pick	■ Concrete retaining wall blocks
■ Posthole digger	■ Concrete adhesive
■ Tamping bar	■ Landscape filter fabric
■ Rubber mallet	■ Mason's line
■ Maul	
■ Mason's chisel	
■ Caulking gun	
■ Electric drill	
■ ⅜" ship-auger bit	

SAFETY TIP

Protect your eyes with goggles when drilling.

EXCAVATING THE SITE

Excavated Earth

Cutting back the slope
Working upward from the base of the slope, cut away the earth along the path of the wall with a pick and shovel. Pitch the excavated soil behind the site of the wall to create a plateau, leaving a drop slightly less than the planned height of the wall.

Setting a level base
Drive stakes to mark the ends of the wall. Stretch a mason's line between the stakes and level the line with a line level. With a shovel and rake, level the soil to a uniform distance under the string all along its length.

Line Level

A MODULAR BLOCK RETAINING WALL

A look behind the wall

Modular block construction eliminates the threat from frost heaves by preventing the buildup of water behind the wall. The mortarless joints allow water to weep through the wall face. The base of the wall consists of 4 inches of compacted and leveled coarse sand. In soils that drain poorly, a 4-inch perforated drain pipe is installed at the level of the first course. Each course is slightly offset from the one beneath it by alignment lips on the blocks. The wall is backfilled with ¾ inch clean drainage aggregate and finished with 3 inches of topsoil. If the soil is very fine, a filter fabric (available at a landscaping supplier) is placed behind the aggregate to keep the backfill clean. Modular block manufacturers recommend heights to which their walls can be built without reinforcement. Always refer to the manufacturer's height guidelines.

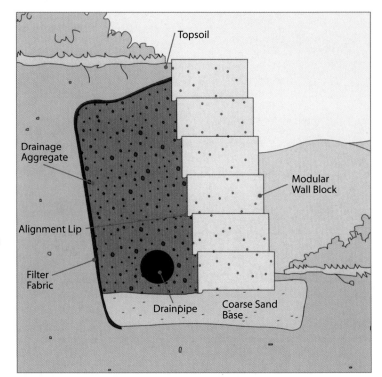

Topsoil

Drainage Aggregate

Modular Wall Block

Alignment Lip

Filter Fabric

Drainpipe

Coarse Sand Base

Alignment Lip

Laying the first course

Dig a shallow trench along the excavated terrace 12 to 18 inches wide and 4 inches deep. If the soil is very fine, spread a layer of filter fabric on the side of the trench, as shown on page 174. Cut the fabric long enough to fold over the aggregate once the top course of blocks is in place. Spread a 4-inch layer of coarse sand in the trench, then compact and level it. Arrange the first course of blocks on the base, digging a shallow trench in the sand to accommodate the alignment lips; align the back face of the blocks with the mason's line you set up when excavating the trench *(page 173)*. Level each block front to back and side to side *(left)*, making sure adjacent units are flush; a rubber mallet can help to position the blocks. To cut a block for the ends and corners, first score it with a mason's chisel and maul. Continue striking with the chisel on all four sides until the block splits.

Backfilling each row

To improve drainage from behind the wall, install a 4-inch perforated plastic drain pipe at the level of the first row of stones, as shown on page 174. Remove the alignment stakes and mason's line, then position the next row of blocks over the first so the alignment lip overhangs the back edge. Overlap the blocks so the joints of the two rows are staggered. Backfill behind each course with ¾-inch drainage aggregate as you proceed *(right)*. Continue adding rows of stones followed by backfill to reach the necessary height.

Securing the top course

Before you lay each block of the last course, apply two beads of concrete adhesive to the blocks in the previous row *(right)*. Fold any filter fabric over the aggregate and fill in the last 2 or 3 inches behind the wall with topsoil.

CONSTRUCTING A PALISADE RETAINING WALL

Digging the trenches

Excavate the wall site *(page 173)*. Dig a trench under the string to a depth equal to the wall height plus 2 inches. Make the trench 4 inches wider than the posts to be used for the wall. Create a flat, even bearing surface on the downhill face of the trench with a square-edged spade *(photograph)*. Starting at one end, use a posthole digger to make a hole for a single timber twice the depth of the trench *(left)*.

Pinning the wall together

Set the corner post in its hole, add gravel to fill the hole, and pack the gravel down with a tamping bar. Dig a shallow trench for four shorter posts next to the first one, set the second post in the trench, and, with a ⅜-inch ship-auger bit, drill two holes, one above grade (left) and one below, through one timber and into the next. If the wood is hard you may need to rent a ½-inch drill, as shown. Drive ⅜-inch reinforcing bars into the holes. Repeat for each short post, staggering the heights of the holes so the bars do not intersect. Add gravel to hold the posts in place. When you have laid and pinned four timbers, make another deep hole with the posthole digger; repeat the procedure for every fifth timber. Fill in the trench with gravel as you go, tamping it down every 4 inches, then fill in the rest of the space between the wall and the retained soil with the soil that was removed.

Fence and Wall Repairs

Even the best-made fence will eventually need repairs. The effects of traffic, weather, and time all take their toll. A few simple fixes, however, can add years to the life of a fence. The commonest problem is rotten wood. Often, most of the board is still sound with only the ends decayed. A quick solution is to support the damaged board with a small block of wood *(opposite)*. A board with more extensive deterioration can be supported by a sister rail *(page 180)*. To ensure your repairs are long-lived, buy pressure-treated wood.

PROBLEMATIC POSTS

A loose post set in soil can often be stabilized by pressing down around the post with a tamping bar. If the post needs added support, bolt on 2-by-4 sister posts *(page 180)*. For a badly damaged post set in soil or concrete, remove and replace the post *(page 181)*.

BRICK WALL REPAIRS

Bricks occasionally need replacement when mortar joints crack or bricks are damaged. A loose brick can usually be worked out of the wall with a pry bar or the end of a cold chisel. A damaged brick may be removed with a cold chisel and a maul. First break the mortar around the brick, then split it into pieces small enough to free with a pry bar.

REBUILDING A STONE WALL

While stones have an indefinite lifespan, stone walls need frequent repair. As the stones settle under their own weight and endure stresses such as frost heaves, sections may collapse. Rebuilding a wall is not complicated but does require patience and lots of trial and error. Remove the stones down to the level where the wall is solid; often this means going right down to the ground. When rebuilding the wall, overlap the stones.

TOOLS	MATERIALS
■ Clamps	■ 2 x 4s, 2 x 6s
■ Hammer	■ 1" plywood
■ Maul	■ Wooden stakes
■ Pliers	■ Galvanized common nails (3", 3 ½")
■ Wrench	■ Galvanized wood screws (1½", 3" No. 8)
■ Screwdriver	
■ Electric drill	■ Carriage bolts (⅜"), washers
■ Screwdriver bit	
■ File	■ Screw eye (½")
■ Handsaw	■ Turnbuckle and wire cable
■ Circular saw	
■ Hacksaw	■ Concrete blocks
■ Pry bar	■ Gravel
■ Tamping bar	
■ Shovel	
■ Posthole digger	
■ Car jack	
■ Stiff-fiber brush	
■ Cold chisel	
■ Pointing trowel	
■ Mason's hawk	

SAFETY TIP

Wear goggles when drilling, work gloves and goggles to chip out mortar, and gloves when working with wet mortar. Wear gloves when handling pressure-treated wood, which contains arsenic compounds as preservatives; add a dust mask when cutting it.

REINFORCING LOOSE FENCE RAILS

Bracing the end of a rail

Cut a block the same width as the rail from a 2-by-4. Drill a pair of ⅛-inch clearance holes through the block so the screws can pass freely through it. Hold the piece of wood in place under the rail and screw it to the post with two 3-inch No. 8 galvanized wood screws *(above)*.

Bracing the length of a rail with a sister rail

Cut off the damaged part of the rail. Cut a length of pressure-treated lumber the same size as the rail—commonly 2-by-4—to fit between the two posts. Position this sister rail underneath the old rail (or above if there is no room below) and clamp it every 12 inches. Toenail the sister to the post on both sides and underneath with 3½-inch galvanized common nails. Bore a ⅜-inch hole through both boards every 18 inches, offsetting them as shown *(right)*. Install ⅜-inch carriage bolts in the holes, then remove the clamps. Fill in the gap in the rail with wood; fasten it with 3-inch galvanized nails.

STRENGTHENING A POST

Steadying a post with sister posts

Cut two pressure-treated 2-by-4s to a length at least half the height of the post to serve as sister posts; saw a 45-degree bevel at one end of each board. Position a sister post, bevel out, against the fence post. Place a scrap 2-by-4 against the top of the sister post and drive the post halfway into the ground with a maul *(left)*. With a circular saw, cut off the top at a 45-degree angle 18 to 24 inches from the ground. In the same way, position and cut the other sister post on the opposite side. Bore two holes through the three posts and secure the sister posts with ⅜-inch carriage bolts. Trim the bolts with a hacksaw *(inset)* and file off any sharp burrs.

REPLACING A POST

Positioning a replacement post
To indicate the location of the old post before removing it, run a string tautly between the posts on either side of the damaged post. Tie a marker string to the line on each side of the post *(left)*. For a corner post, extend a line from both lengths of fence, past the corner post and secure each one to a stake *(inset)*.

Removing the old post
Remove the rails and fencing on both sides of the post. Loosen the post and footing, if any, by removing the earth around the post with a shovel and a posthole digger, then rock the post back and forth. Install the replacement post as you would a new one, then reinstall the rails and fencing. If the post is too heavy to be lifted out by one or two people—especially if it is set in concrete—enlist the help of a car jack. Nail a 12-inch 2-by-4 to the post and nail a 2-by-6 under it, resting one end on the car jack and the other on a pair of concrete blocks *(right)*. Support the car jack, and with a helper guiding the post, raise it with the jack.

Jack

2 x 4

2 x 6

Concrete Footing

REPAIRING SAGGING GATES

Brace

Rail

Bracing with wood

Prop a block under the latch side of the gate to hold it in its correct closed position. Tack a brace the same dimensions as the rails diagonally across the top and bottom rails, and mark cut lines on its back along the rails *(above)*. Cut the brace at the marks. Position the brace between the rails, bore clearance and pilot holes 1 inch from each end *(inset)*, and drive 1½-inch No. 8 galvanized wood screws into the rail. Also drive a 1-inch screw into every other picket. If the gate still sags, try correcting it with a wire and tumbuckle stay *(opposite)*.

Wire
Clamp

Turnbuckle

Wire-and-
Turnbuckle
Stay

Bracing with a wire-and-turnbuckle stay

Open a 3-inch turnbuckle to its full extension and attach a length of cable to each end with a wire clamp *(inset)*. The cable length will vary with the size of the gate. Fasten a ½-inch screw eye to the corner of the top rail on the hinge side and the opposite corner of the bottom rail as shown, then attach the ends of the turnbuckle wires. Trim any excess wire with pliers. Tighten the turnbuckle to pull the gate back into square *(above)*.

REFITTING A MISSING STONE IN A DRY-LAID WALL

Wedges

Placing a stone in a tight spot

You may be able to insert the stone by hand. If a little extra force is required, tap the stone in place with a maul, cushioning the blows with a wood block. Otherwise, enlarge the opening with the help of wood or metal wedges. With a maul, drive a wedge between the stone directly above the opening and the stones on either side of the opening. Drive in as many wedges as needed to enlarge the opening enough to reposition the missing stone. Insert the stone *(above)* and pull out the wedges.

REBUILDING A DRY-LAID WALL

Recreating a section of wall from the ground up

To rebuild part of a wall, remove a V-shaped section that extends as far down as necessary. Unless the stones are damaged in the second tier behind the first, leave those stones intact. Number the stones with chalk in the order you plan to remove them to make rebuilding easier *(above, left)*. Working with a helper to lift the heavier units, start removing stones at least 2 feet to either side of the damaged area. A pry bar will help release any stubborn stones. To lower heavy stones, lay a 2-by-6 against the wall and slide them down it. If you go down as far as the ground, make a tamper by fastening a 1-inch-thick piece of plywood to a 2-by-4. Tamp the ground *(above, right)*, adding gravel if necessary to make it level with the surrounding earth. Replace the stones, reversing the order in which they were removed. Seat each stone securely on the one below it, using small stones as shims if necessary. Work carefully to replace the top tier of stones; these capstones are twice as wide as the lower-tier units—and twice as heavy. Try tilting them into position, rather than placing them down flat. Fit small stones under them if necessary.

Setting Fence Posts

The key to an attractive, long-lasting fence is a row of sturdy fence posts, securely anchored and properly aligned and spaced. Posts are the working members of a fence, serving to bear and brace the gates and railings.

There is a wide range of fence post materials, as shown in the box opposite. Before setting any posts, check your property line and local zoning or building codes, which may determine fence height or setback from the street.

To help protect the top of a fence from rain, cut the post at a 30-to 45-degree angle before setting it, or cover it with a plastic or metal post cap, available at home centers to fit standard post sizes.

SETTING POSTS STRAIGHT AND SECURE

As a general rule, one-third of the post should be below ground. In relatively stable soil, tamped earth or gravel will hold the post securely. Gateposts as well as the end and corner posts, which are subjected to greater stress, should be set in concrete wherever possible. If you prefer not to go to the trouble and expense of using concrete, use longer lengths of lumber for these key posts and sink them deeper into the ground.

Avoid leaving holes unattended; set a post in its hole as soon as possible or at least mark the hazard by inserting the post or a tall stake.

SAFETY TIP

Wear gloves when handling pressure-treated lumber; add a dust mask when cutting it.

OVERCOMING FROST HEAVES

As freezing water expands under and around posts, it tends to force them up. One solution is to sink the post below the frost line, which varies from region to region. It is generally impractical to sink posts deeper than 3 to 3½ feet. In this case, set the post in concrete; nails partly driven into the post help to hold it to the concrete. For added stability first widen the hole at the base into a bell shape so the surrounding earth holds the concrete in place.

Whether or not you use concrete, always set the base of the post in 6 inches of gravel. The improved drainage reduces the risks of frost heaves and prevents the post bottom from resting in groundwater and rotting. Four ways to set a post are shown on page 192.

TOOLS	MATERIALS
■ Carpenter's level	■ 1 x 2
■ Line level	■ Wooden stakes
■ Plumb bob	■ Common nails (1½")
■ 1 x 2 gauge pole	■ Gravel
■ Hammer	■ Pre-mixed concrete
■ Maul	■ Mason's line
■ Handsaw	
■ Mason's trowel	
■ Shovel	
■ Garden spade	
■ Posthole digger	
■ Tamping bar	

AN ARRAY OF POST MATERIALS

Mortised
Cedar Post

Plain
Cedar Post

PVC Post

Treated
6 x 6

Treated
4 x 4

Pressure-treated lumber is one of the most popular choices for fence posts, and with good reason: They are strong, widely available, and last at least 20 years. But there are other sound options. Naturally resistant woods like redwood, red and white cedar, and locust are all good choices if they are available for a good price in your area. They are commonly used for rustic-style fences. PVC posts, although more costly than wood, are attractive and typically guaranteed to last a lifetime.

Most wood fences are best supported by posts no smaller than 4-by-4s, but low picket fences can be anchored with 2-by-4 posts. All corner and gateposts should be 4-by-4s or larger.

LAYING OUT THE POSTS

Locating posts on flat ground

Drive stakes at the locations of the end posts and stretch a mason's line between them. Measure the distance between the posts and determine the standard lengths of lumber or fencing that will make up the rails of the fence with a minimum of cutting. In general, posts are spaced a maximum of 8 feet apart; this way, a 16-foot length of lumber will span three posts. Make a gauge pole by cutting a straight 1-by-2 board to the length of the fence sections. Lay out the post positions with stakes as shown at left. Adjust the intervals for gateposts and to avoid ending the fence with a very short section.

End Stake

Mason's
Line

Gauge
Pole

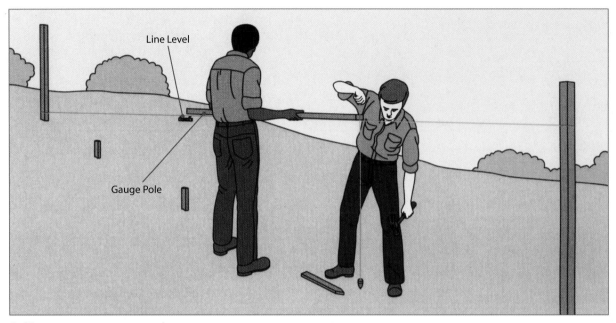

Line Level

Gauge Pole

Staking posts on uneven ground

For a fence with a level top, stretch a mason's line between two end stakes and level it with a line level. With a helper measuring along the line with a gauge pole, drop a plumb bob from the line to pinpoint each post location on the ground *(above)*. Drive a stake at each one. For a fence that follows the contours of the ground, drive stakes at the fence ends and at each high and low point in between. Join all the stakes with a mason's line and position the stakes for the remaining posts evenly along the line as shown above.

MARKING A SQUARE CORNER

This simple method has been used to lay out right angles for centuries. Drive stakes to establish your first fence line, with one stake at the desired comer point. Attach a mason's line to these two stakes, then tie a marker string to the line at the 3-foot mark. Stretch another line from the corner stake, roughly perpendicular to the first line and secure it to a batter board—a horizontal board nailed to two stakes. Tie a marker string to this line at the 4-foot mark. Slide this line along the batter board so that the distance between the two marker strings is 5 feet *(right)*. The angle between the two lines will be 90 degrees.

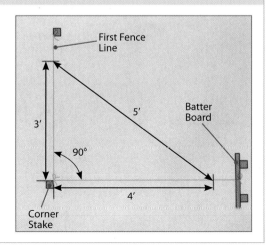

First Fence Line

3'

5'

90°

4'

Batter Board

Corner Stake

DIGGING POSTHOLES

Burrowing a hole with a posthole digger

Untie the mason's line from the stakes, putting it aside for aligning the posts *(page 191)*. Start the hole by cutting out a circle of sod around the stake with a spade. Dig out the posthole with a clamshell posthole digger, as shown. For very sandy or heavy clay soils, a digger like the one shown in the photograph works best. A post set in concrete requires a hole three times the post width; for one to be set in tamped earth make the hole twice the post width. If the frost line is deeper than 3 feet angle the digger to widen the bottom *(above)*. Extend the hole 6 inches deeper than needed and pour in 6 inches of gravel.

A HOLE-DIGGING TIMESAVER

Depth Marker

If you are setting 10 or more fence posts, consider renting a power auger. Unless you are working in very rocky or very heavy clay soils it saves both time and effort. The two-person auger above is less likely to kick out of the hole when it hits a rock than the one-person version.

To use a power auger, mark the posthole depth on the bit with tape and set the machine over the marked position. Start the motor and adjust the speed with the handle-mounted throttle. Guide the machine as the bit pulls it into the ground. After digging 8 to 12 inches, raise the bit to clear the dirt from the hole. If you hit a rock, pry it loose with a digging bar or pick and shovel.

ALIGNING FENCE POSTS

Bracing an end or corner post

Drive two stakes on adjacent sides of the posthole. Fasten a 1-by-2-inch bracing board to each stake with a single 1½-inch common nail. Center a post in the hole and use a carpenter's level to plumb one side of the post *(left)*; alternatively, use a special post level *(photograph)*, which will enable you to plumb both directions at once. Nail the first brace to the post, then check for plumb on the other side and secure the second brace.

Aligning intermediate posts

Attach two lines to the end posts, one near the top and the other close to ground level. For the upper line, make sure that it is attached at exactly the same distance from the top of the posts. Place an intermediate post in a hole. Add or remove gravel to set the post at the correct height according to the alignment line. Have a helper align one side of the intermediate post with the two lines, then plumb an adjacent side with a level. Sight along the top line to check both the post height and the alignment *(right)*; alter alignment by shifting the post base.

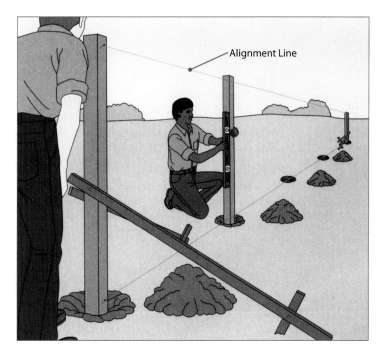

Alignment Line

FOUR WAYS TO PLANT A POST

There is no one correct way to secure a fence post. Soil type, intended use, climate, and budget all influence the selection of fillers. The one ingredient common to all methods is a 6-inch base of gravel. This will help prevent water from pooling around the post bottom where it will be drawn into the end grain and hasten decay.

The simplest method is to replace and tamp the soil that was removed to make the hole. This works well if the fence is less than 4 feet high and sitting in well-drained soil, which reduces the risk of frost heave.

There are two practical reasons to bolster a post with concrete: strength and protection from frost heave. If additional strength is needed but frost heave is not a significant threat, then fill the hole halfway with tamped soil and top it with concrete, for a partial concrete collar. If the post only requires protection against frost heave, then pour enough concrete to fill the bottom 8 to 12 inches of the hole, driving nails partway into the post to anchor it to the concrete.

A full concrete collar, extending from the drainage gravel to just above the ground, is definitely the strongest method of setting a post. It protects against frost heave and will render a post strong enough to hang a gate or hold a tall fence.

FITTING A HOLE FOR A CROOKED POST

Unmilled round posts of cedar, locust, or redwood are often curved at their large end. To allow for this, dig the hole to the correct depth; then shape one side to match the curve on the post, allowing the above-ground part of the post to stand plumb. Finally, dig the hole 6 inches deeper, then add 6 inches of gravel for drainage. When the earth is tamped back in place the post will be directly braced against undisturbed soil, providing a secure support.

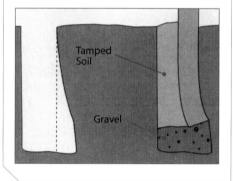

Tamped Soil

Gravel

Securing a post in tamped earth
While a helper holds the post plumb and touching the alignment lines *(page 29)* fill the hole with earth in 3- to 4-inch layers, tamping as you go with the flat end of a tamping bar or a 2-by-4. Make sure you do not inadvertently shift the position of the post. If you are using only soil, overfill the hole and shape a slope of earth around the post to shed runoff. If you are topping the hole with concrete, simply fill the hole to the appropriate height with tamped earth, leaving room for the concrete *(opposite)*.

Setting a post in concrete
Ensure that the post is aligned and plumb.
Prepare a batch of premixed concrete with a
square-edged spade according to the manufacturer's
directions, then fill the hole. Agitate the concrete
with the shovel to remove any air pockets, but
be careful not to knock the post out of position.
Overfill the hole slightly and use a mason's trowel to
slope the concrete down from the post to improve
runoff. Allow the concrete to set for 48 hours before
removing the braces or attaching the fencing.
If you are only laying down a concrete anchor,
pour in about 8 to 12 inches of concrete; usually
this amounts to one bag of pre-mixed concrete for
each post.

Wooden Fences

Almost every wooden fence is built on a framework of upright posts and connecting rails, or stringers. This simple skeleton can support a range of fences that will meet practically any need. A fence of nothing more than posts and rails makes a clear boundary marker, adapts well to rough or rolling terrain, and covers the most ground with the least lumber. Siding nailed to a post-and-stringer frame can take the shape of a low picket fence to decorate the border of a front yard or of a tall board fence *(page 203)* to ensure privacy or keep children and pets within bounds.

BUILDING MATERIALS

In all of these fence styles, your first concern is the quality of the building materials. Assemble the fence with pressure-treated lumber or naturally decay-and insect-resistant woods, such as cedar or redwood. All are more expensive than construction-grade lumber, but they will last longer. Fasten the elements with hot-dipped galvanized, aluminum, or stainless-steel fasteners, which will not rust and stain the fence.

SAFETY TIP

Protect your eyes when hammering nails, using a circular saw, or operating a router. Wear gloves when handling pressure-treated lumber, and add a dust mask when cutting it.

POST-AND-BOARD FENCES

The fence of this type shown on the following pages is made of 1-by lumber, face-nailed to 4-by-4 posts. For a three-rail fence, set the posts 36 to 42 inches high. For a four-rail fence, make the posts 48 to 54 inches high. To protect the top ends of posts from rot, top them with plastic or metal caps or with an angled cap rail.

PICKET FENCES

This type of fence is built in a wide range of styles. If you cannot find prefabricated pickets you will have to cut your own. A picket fence can be any height but is usually 3 to 4 feet, with l-by-4 pickets projecting about 6 inches above the top stringer.

The tops of picket fences can be cut into any number of original shapes. The best tool for a relatively short fence is a saber saw or, for mass production, a router equipped with a flush-trimming bit.

POST-AND-RAIL FENCES

With tapered rail ends that fit into mortised posts, these fences are sturdier than post-and-board fences and almost as easy to install. With this fence style, the posts are not all set first—they are placed in their holes as the fence is assembled. Prefabricated mortised posts and tapered stringers are sold by lumber suppliers in a variety of styles.

TOOLS

- Tape measure
- Carpenter's level
- Combination square
- Carpenter's square
- Clamps
- Hammer
- Maul
- Tamping bar
- Drawknife

- Handsaw
- Circular saw
- Saber saw
- Electric drill
- Screwdriver bit
- ¾" spade bit
- Drill guide
- Drill-press stand
- Router and flush-trimming bit

MATERIALS

- Fence posts and rails
- 1 x 4s, 1 x 6s
- 2 x 3s, 2 x 4s
- Wooden stakes
- Dowels (¾")
- Galvanized common nails (2½", 3½")
- Galvanized wood screws (1¼" No. 6; ¾", 2½" No. 8)
- Angle irons

- Mason's line
- Sandpaper (medium grade)
- Wood glue (exterior)

A SIMPLE POST-AND-BOARD FENCE

Spacer

Post Cap

Second Line Post

First Line Post

Building a post-and-board fence

Trim a 1-by-4 or 1-by-6 to extend from a corner or end post to the center of the second line post. Nail this board to the posts with 2½-inch galvanized common nails. Trim the board for the next course so it fits from the corner to the center of the first line post, then nail it in place with the aid of a spacer cut to the appropriate length *(above)*. This will result in staggered joints that will make for a more rigid fence. Work toward the opposite corner, attaching boards cut to span three posts until you need short pieces for ends. Finally, nail metal or plastic caps onto the posts.

THE FINISHED LOOK OF A CAP RAIL

Beveling the posts

Prepare each post for the cap rail by sawing a 30-degree bevel at the post's top end before you set the post in the ground. Set your circular saw to cut a 30-degree angle across the post about 3 inches from one end *(above, left)*. The saw will cut only partway

through and you must finish with a handsaw. To prepare a corner post, make a second cut at a 30-degree angle across an adjacent side *(above, right)*. To set the posts, refer to the instructions on page 192.

Line Post

Corner Post

Marking the cap rail

With a helper, hold a 1-by-6 in position on top of a corner post and a line post. Have the helper set one end of the board at the center of the line post while you mark the underside of the board along the angle of the top of the corner post *(left)*. Mark the matching cap-rail board to fit across the other angled face of the corner post. With a combination square, transfer the marks to the other face of each board to facilitate sawing.

Cutting the cap rail

Set your circular saw to cut a 30-degree angle. Saw the rails along the marks you made in the previous step *(right)*. Fasten one of the cap rails with 2½-inch galvanized common nails to the corner post and line post, aligning the tops of the rails with the top edges of the beveled posts. Place the other cap rail in position and test the fit *(inset)*. If necessary, trim the board with a block plane.

A BASIC PICKET FENCE

Mitered Ends

Stringer

Corner Post

Line Post

Angle Iron

Installing the stringers

Stringers can be installed face down as shown or on edge. The former method is more prone to sag under the weight of the fence while the latter one is more likely to bow from wind pressure. For the bottom stringers, trim 2-by-4s to fit between each pair of posts and secure an angle iron to each end with 34-inch galvanized No. 8 wood screws. Attach these stringers to the posts about 8 inches above the ground: Drive screws through the angle iron and toenail the 2-by-4s with 3½-inch galvanized common nails. Cut the first top stringer to length to stretch from the corner post to the middle of the first line post. Miter one end of the board at 45 degrees so it will match the stringer on the adjoining fence line. Drill two clearance holes in each end of the stringer, then fasten it to the posts with 2½-inch No. 8 wood screws (left). Continue to install stringers in this way, using long 2-by-4s to span as many posts as possible. Cut the pattern in the top of your pickets (below); if you have purchased precut pickets, go ahead and attach them.

TEMPLATES FOR PICKET PATTERNS

From the simple rounded shape to more complicated patterns, the gallery above shows just a sample of the possible forms of picket tops you can cut yourself. The first step is to design the pattern on paper. Then transfer it to a 1-by-4 board and cut out the shape with a saber saw. Sand any rough spots. You can use this as a template to draw the pattern on the picket stock before cutting out each one with a saber saw (page 200). A faster method would be to cut the shape out of ½-inch plywood and use it as a router template (page 201).

Cutting a pattern freehand

Outline the template pattern onto a picket, then clamp the picket to a work table. To keep the saber-saw blade from binding in the kerf, make release cuts from the edge of the picket to the tightest turns. Align the blade with the beginning of the cutting line, then feed the saw into the stock, guiding the tool to keep the blade on line (*right*). Smooth any rough spots on the picket with medium-grade sandpaper.

Template

Release
Cuts

Spacer

Cleat

Attaching the pickets

Make a spacer to help you set the height and spacing of the pickets: Cut a piece of scrap wood to the same length as the pickets, then rip it to the desired width of the gap between the pickets. Attach a cleat to the spacer so it will hang from the top stringer at the correct height. Drill two clearance holes in each picket at the spots where they will contact the stringers. Set the first picket against the edge of an end post and align its point with the top of the spacer. Plumb the picket with a level and secure it with a 1¼-inch No. 6 screw. Continue in this manner (*above*), checking with a level every few pickets to make sure they are not straying out of plumb.

SHAPING PICKETS WITH A ROUTER

Bearing

Template

Picket

Cutting along the template

Outline the template *(page 199)* on the picket, then cut out the pattern roughly with a saber saw staying about ¼ inch outside the line. Align the template over the picket stock and clamp the assembly to a work surface. Fit the router with a top-piloted flush-trimming bit and adjust the cutting depth so the bearing will be in line with the template. To make the cut, slide the router toward the picket until the bearing touches the template. Move the router around the picket against the direction of bit rotation, keeping the bearing pressed against the template.

A LONG-LASTING ALTERNATIVE: VINYL FENCING

Vinyl fencing offers several advantages over the traditional wooden version, the main one being longevity. Most manufacturers offer at least a 20-year warranty on their fences; some even guarantee them for the life of the original owner. Available in a huge variety of styles, vinyl fencing requires little upkeep. And at the end of its useful life, it is 100 percent recyclable. All these advantages come at a price: vinyl fencing may cost more than a comparable wood fence. However, in the long run, the maintenance-free nature of the product can make it an economical option.

PLAIN PICKETS IN A CURVED PATTERN

Building panels of pickets

Panel frames are built of 2-by-3s so that the pickets
will fall flush with the outer face of a 4-by-4 post.
If you want a stronger frame and do not mind the
pickets sticking out a little from the posts, use 2-by-4s.
Build rectangular frames of 2-by-3s to fit between
each pair of posts. For each frame, cut pickets to the
length of your longest picket and drill clearance holes
where they will cross the stringers. Plan to situate
the bottom stringers 8 inches above the ground. Lay
one picket in the middle of the frame and check it for
squareness to the stringers with a carpenter's square.
Lay out the remaining pickets evenly spaced, and mark
their locations on the frames. Secure the pickets with
1¼-inch No. 6 galvanized wood screws.

End Nail

Marking a curved pattern

On the first panel, measure down from the top center picket the desired depth
of the curve and drive a nail. Drive two end nails at the top of the picket panel,
each a distance from the central nail equal to half the panel length. Tie a length
of mason's line to one end nail, pull it around the central nail, and fasten it to the
other end nail. Remove the middle nail. Keeping the line taut, pull a pencil along
it to draw a curve on the picket panel *(above)*. Mark each panel this way and cut
the curves with a saber saw.

Installing the panels

Position a panel between the posts. Rest it on a pair
of 4-by-4 blocks so the tallest picket is at the desired
height. Clamp the panel to the post at each end. Drill
several clearance holes into the frame then fasten it to
the post with 2½-inch No. 8 wood screws *(above)*. If the
panel sags over time, add another 2-by-3 under the top
one, positioned on edge with its face against the pickets.

Tall Fences for Privacy

Most privacy fences are built like the picket fences shown on pages 199 to 200. Standard pressure-treated lumber nailed to simple post-and-stringer frames will yield a variety of attractive fences; prefabricated panels can be nailed directly to posts or framed inside posts and stringers.

Tall fences are typically supported on frames of 4-by-4 posts and 2-by-4 stringers. The simplest privacy fence is made of vertical boards or tall narrow slats nailed directly to the top and bottom stringers (and to a middle stringer if the fence is taller than 6 feet). Almost as simple is a fence of horizontal boards or plywood panels face-nailed to the posts and to 2-by-4 studs that are toenailed to the top and bottom stringers 24 to 36 inches apart.

STRENGTHENING THE FENCE

Since the stringers are attached face down, the fence is weaker than if the boards were set on edge. To compensate for this, use the lightest possible materials and reduce the distance between posts to 6 feet or less. Another approach is to screw an extra 2-by-4 on edge underneath one or both of the stringers.

WORKING WITH A ROUTER

When routing in tandem with a jig, clamp or nail the jig to the workpiece and make sure the lumber is steady. Keep the router at chest height or below. To make the high cuts in the posts, stand on a stepladder steadied by a helper.

TOOLS

- T-bevel
- Combination square
- Water level
- Clamps
- Hammer
- Screwdriver
- Circular saw
- Router and ¾" straight bit
- Paintbrush

MATERIALS

- 1 x 2s, 1 x 4s, 1 x 6s
- 2 x 4s, 2 x 6s
- Galvanized common nails (2", 3½")
- Wood screws (1¼" No. 6)
- Wood glue (exterior)
- Wood preservative

SAFETY TIP

Put on goggles when routing. Wear gloves when handling pressure-treated lumber; add a dust mask when cutting it.

Board-and-Board

Basket Weave

Three screens for your yard

A board-and-board fence admits a breeze and looks good from either side. Vertical boards are nailed to both sides of the frame, separated by less than their own widths. The thin slats (½-by-6 inch) that make up a basket weave fence are woven around vertical 1-by-1 boards, and fastened in vertical grooves on each post. The boards on one side are positioned opposite the spaces on the other. Ready-made panels in elaborate styles like latticework are mounted against 1-by-2s nailed to the posts and stringers.

Lattice Panel

Adapting to Uneven Ground

Building a fence that follows the ups and downs of your property often depends on choosing the right style of fence for your land and modifying the design as necessary. A post-and-rail or post-and-board fence *(page 196)* conforms to any terrain and is best for sharply sloping or rolling ground; a fence with vertical members face-nailed to a post-and-board frame follows the ground almost as well.

PICKETS ALONG THE SLOPE

On rough but relatively level ground, a fence with pickets or slats *(page 206)* can smooth out small dips and rises; its bottom follows the earth's contours while the top remains level. For such a fence, buy enough long pickets to fill in the low spots.

ADAPTING RECTANGULAR PANELS

Rectangular-paneled fences are not suited for rough or rolling ground, but they adapt well to steady slopes if built in steps *(page 207)*. Uniform stepping requires a few calculations, but once the posts are in position, attaching stringers and siding is straightforward.

Normally, the top of each fence section is set level. But on a steep hill this can create the illusion that the section is actually higher on the downhill end. In this case, some fence builders lower the downhill end of the stringer 1 or 2 inches below level until it looks right.

TOOLS	MATERIALS
■ Tape measure	■ Mason's line
■ Carpenter's level	
■ Line level or water level	
■ Plumb bob	
■ Clamps	
■ Hammer	
■ Circular saw	

SAFETY TIP

Wear safety goggles when hammering.

Level

Going up and down hills

Set posts on each rise and in each depression, then space the remaining posts between them. For a post-and-board fence like the one shown, clamp or tack the boards in position against the posts and use a level to make vertical marks on the boards at the post centers wherever two boards meet *(above)*. Trim the boards at the marked angles. Before attaching vertical slats or pickets, align them evenly above the top stringer with a spacer *(page 196)* then plumb each one.

Leveling bumps and dips

Make a spacer as shown on page 200. To line up pickets on uneven ground, hold each one upside down against the stringers with its shaped top ½ inches off the ground. Mark its bottom end even with the top of the spacer *(left)*, then trim to the mark. Install the pickets as you would for a standard picket fence *(page 200)*.

Spacer

Upside-Down Picket

SCRIBING THE PICKET BOTTOM FOR A CLOSE FIT

While a picket fence does not have to follow the exact profile of the ground, incorporating this feature is a nice professional touch. Simply trim the pickets to length using the method shown above, but let the pickets touch the ground. Place them in position against the fence, right-side up. Hold a carpenter's pencil on a short piece of scrap 2-by-4 *(right)*. Slide the block along the ground to scribe any variation in the terrain on the bottom of the picket. Trim the picket with a saber saw. The gap between the pickets and the ground will be uniform all along the fence.

Post

Stringer Drop

Stringer

Stepping down a slope

Run a level line from the top of the hill to a tall stake at the bottom *(page 191)*. The height of the line on the bottom stake is the hill's vertical drop. Lay out the fence line and mark the post locations as shown on page 191. Divide the number of fence sections into the total vertical drop to calculate the "stringer drop" from one section to the next. Set the first post at the top of the hill to the intended fence height, and the rest of the posts to the fence height plus the stringer drop. Mark the stringer drops on the posts, then attach the stringers *(page 199)*. For a fence with vertical boards, trim each one so its bottom conforms to the slope, the top is even with the top stringer, and there is a 1½-inch gap between the board and the ground *(left)*.

Building Gates

Gates lead a tough life and most show it by eventually sagging, binding, and refusing to latch. But by observing three basic rules you can greatly increase the useful life of your gate.

GATEPOSTS AND BRACES

The first requirement is a pair of strong, plumb gateposts, set in concrete *(page 194)* to a depth equal to one-half the height of the part above-ground. Space the posts to accommodate the gate width plus a ½-inch clearance for the latch as well as enough clearance for the kind of hinge you plan to install.

The second critical element is a frame that is braced by a diagonal board between the top rail at the latch side and the bottom rail at the hinge side. To provide bottom clearance, hang all gates at least 2 inches above the highest point of ground within the arc of the opening gate.

HARDWARE

Choose strong hardware, particularly the hinges; weak hinges are the most frequent cause of gate problems. To prevent rusting, use stainless steel or galvanized items.

Among latches, the simplest and most trouble-free is the self-latching type shown on page 211; sliding bolts are not recommended because even a slight sag in the gate will throw them out of alignment. A gate spring can be added to automatically close the gate.

TOOLS

- Tape measure
- Carpenter's square
- Hammer
- Screwdriver
- Awl or large nail
- Circular saw
- Electric drill
- Screwdriver bit

MATERIALS

- 1" x 1½" board
- Pressure-treated 2 x 4s
- Pickets
- Galvanized common nails (3")
- Galvanized wood screws (1¼" No. 6; 1", 4" No. 8)
- Lag screws (⁵⁄₁₆") and washers
- Gate hinges
- Gate latch

SAFETY TIP

Wear goggles when drilling. Wear gloves when handling pressure-treated lumber; add a dust mask when cutting.

Strap Hinge

T-Hinge

Screw-Hook Hinge

Three types of hinges

These three styles of hinge attach to the gate with a strap at least 7 inches long but they differ in the way they are secured to the post. The strap- and T-hinges are fastened to the post and gate with lag screws; screw-hook hinges are fixed with screw hooks. The strap hinge has a post strap running the full width of the post. The T-hinge has at least a 7-inch-high strap, which makes it more stable. The screw-hook hinge is even stronger and makes the gate easy to remove for minor repairs.

MAKING AND HANGING A GATE

Rail

Assembling the frame

Cut pressure-treated 2-by-4s the width of the gate for rails. Position the end pickets so that the gate rails and pickets will align with the fence. Drill clearance holes in the pickets. Screw the pickets to the rail with 1¼-inch No. 6 galvanized wood screws, checking with a carpenter's square to guarantee right angles *(left)*. For a fence 6 feet tall or more, add a third rail in the middle of the frame.

Bracing the gate

Turn the gate over picket-side down. Position a 2-by-4 brace on the gate from the top corner on the latch side to the bottom corner on the hinge side. Mark the 2-by-4 to fit between the rails, aligning a straightedge with each rail *(right)*. Cut the brace to length. Drill two clearance holes through the edge of the brace about 2 inches in from each end, then secure it with 4-inch No. 8 wood screws. Secure the remaining pickets to the rails and the brace. Bolt the hinge straps to the ends of the rails with ⅝-inch lag screws.

Brace

Clearance Hole

Hanging the gate

Set the gate on wood blocks to align it with the fence and, holding the back of the frame flush with the back of the post, mark the post at the bottom of both hinges *(left)*. Bore a ½-inch-diameter hole in the corner of the post at a 45-degree angle, starting the hole with an awl or large nail so the drill will not slip off the corner. With the hook set at an angle *(inset)* the gate can swing a full 180 degrees without binding against the post. Drive the screw hooks into the post. Slip the hinge straps over the screw hooks to hang the gate.

Screw Hook

Installing a latch and a gate spring

Position the latch on the post opposite the top rail on the gate. Secure the hardware with 1-inch No. 8 wood screws. Hold the gate closed and fit the bar in the latch, pressing it against the rail as it would normally sit. Mark the screw holes with a pencil, then drill a pair of pilot holes. Fasten the bar to the gate with 1-inch wood screws *(above)*. To make a gate stop, nail a 1-by-1½ board to the front of the latch post with 3-inch galvanized common nails, positioned so the gate will stop just before the bar strikes the base of the latch. This will keep the latch from bearing the brunt of the force when the gate is closed. To operate the latch from outside the gate, first bore a hole through the post, then attach a cord to the hole in the latch bar, thread it through the post, and tie a pull ring to the cord on the other side of the post. If you want to add a gate spring, set it across the gate post and gate in as vertical a position as possible so the movable bracket is on top and tilted to the right. Mark and drill pilot holes, then fasten the spring in place with the screws supplied *(inset)*. Tighten the spring by turning the hex nut at the top clockwise, then fit the metal stop between the nut and bracket to prevent the nut from loosening.

Blocks and Bricks for a Strong High Wall

Because of its solidity and weight, a masonry wall calls for very careful planning. It must sit on soil firm enough to support it, and not block natural drainage. If you have any doubts about the site of your wall, consult your local building authority. In many areas, codes prescribe strict standards for masonry structures more than a few feet high, specifying materials, dimensions, reinforcement, and depths of footings.

DIGGING TRENCHES FOR FOOTINGS

The footings must be at least 18 inches below grade and must rest on earth not affected by frost. Before digging, mark the borders of the footing trench and the centerline of the wall with stakes clear of the digging area to fix the marks. In loose soil, you may have to bank the trench walls back from the bed by as much as 45 degrees to keep them from caving in. Keep the bed as level and flat as you can, but do not smooth it off by filling loose earth back in: The footing must rest on undisturbed earth. If the virgin soil at the proper depth is loose, tamp it.

A footing's width and height depend on the thickness of the structure it supports and local soil conditions; consult your building code.

POURING CONCRETE FOOTINGS

In any but the loosest soil, wooden forms are not needed to contain the concrete poured for a footing. In most soils, widen the trench on one side to allow for smoothing the concrete and laying blocks and mortar from the footing up to the surface (opposite, left). But if the soil is firm enough to keep the trench walls vertical for their full height, you have a convenient but expensive alternative: You can dig the trench no wider than the footing and fill it with concrete to just below ground level (opposite, right).

Both types of footing need strengthening with two lines of steel reinforcing bars (rebar) laid along the trench—and both probably need enough concrete for an order from a ready-mix firm. When the truck arrives, have plenty of helpers on hand. Pouring and leveling concrete is heavy work that must be done quickly.

TOOLS	MATERIALS
■ Tape measure	■ 2 x 4s for floats
■ 4' level	■ Wooden stakes
■ Water level	■ Common nails (4½")
■ Hammer	■ Rebar
■ Maul	■ Tie wire
■ Rebar cutter	■ Sand
■ Square-edged shovel	■ Bricks or stones
	■ Ready-mix concrete
	■ Polyethylene sheeting

SAFETY TIP

Check with utility companies about pipe and wire locations before digging a wall's foundation. Wear gloves and a long-sleeved shirt when working with concrete.

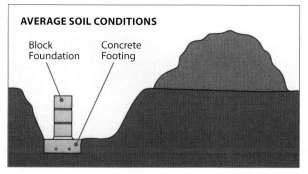

AVERAGE SOIL CONDITIONS

Block
Foundation

Concrete
Footing

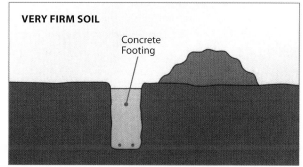

VERY FIRM SOIL

Concrete
Footing

Two types of concrete footing

A standard trench *(above, left)* is suitable for most soils. One of its walls is as steep as the firmness of the soil allows; the bottom is squared off to the width and depth of the footing, and above that the trench gets a foot or two wider to create working space. Reinforcing bars are laid, concrete is poured and leveled, then a block foundation is built up to within a few inches of ground level. A trench dug in very firm soil *(above, right)*, has vertical walls separated by the width of the footing. Reinforcement is laid and the trench is filled with concrete almost to the surface; it needs no block foundation.

POURING A CONCRETE FOOTING

Footing Trench

Marking the top of the footing

Dig the trench for the footing. If you must move a large amount of soil to dig beyond the frost line and you plan to build a high wall more than a dozen feet long, hire a professional. To move a relatively small amount of earth, consider renting a gasoline-powered trencher, which you can operate yourself. Along the sides of the footing trench, drive 12-inch stakes into the ground in a zigzag pattern every 3 to 4 feet. Mark the stake at the highest spot in the trench, 8 to 10 inches above the bed. Mark all the stakes at that height with the help of a water level *(left)*.

Grade Peg

Installing grade pegs

Make grade pegs by cutting a rebar into 18-inch lengths, one for each stake, with a rented rebar cutter. Drive a peg into the trench bed next to each stake so that the top of the peg is level with the mark on the stake *(above)*. Do not drive the pegs too deep—pulling them up to the correct height will loosen them. Remove the stakes as you go, filling in the holes they leave with soil. Check the level of the pegs with a 4-foot level. If any is too high, tap it down.

Reinforcing Bar

Laying reinforcing bars

Check your building code for the correct size rebar—usually between No. 4 and No. 8. Set lengths of rebar in the trench bed alongside each row of grade pegs, supporting the bars 2 to 3 inches above the soil with bricks or stones. Where two bars meet end to end, overlap them 12 to 15 inches. Cut bars to length if necessary with a rebar cutter. Lash the bars together with tie wire, then tie the bars to the grade pegs. Once all the bars are in place, remove the bricks or stones.

Completing the footing

Working with helpers, pour concrete into the trench, taking care not to dislodge the grade pegs. Spread the concrete with square-edged shovels. Break up large air pockets in the concrete by pushing a shovel into the mix, again avoiding the grade pegs. Fill the trench so that the level of the concrete is at least ½ inch above the tops of the grade pegs. Level the footing with floats fashioned from 2-by-4s nailed together *(right)*. Working on one small area at a time, even out the concrete with a patting motion. Continue, compacting the concrete and spreading it into the corners of the trench until the tops of the grade pegs become visible. Smooth out the concrete by sweeping the trailing edge of the float across the surface, pulling the float toward you in wide arcs. Again, continue until the tops of the grade pegs and footing are at the same level. Cover the footing with polyethylene sheeting and let it cure for seven days.

Designing a Wall for Strength and Beauty

Masonry walls need not always present a solid, unvarying face. Bricks and masonry blocks can be laid in patterns to enliven a wall's appearance and in open designs to admit light and air while screening a view.

BUILDING WITH BLOCKS AND BRICK

The decorative block patterns shown opposite feature stacked bond and blocks of standard sizes. Bricks, too, can also be used to make open work, but such walls require a skilled mason to make them structurally sound. An amateur bricklayer, however, can build a solid-brick wall with a decorative pattern based on the interplay of headers (bricks laid crosswise on the wall) and stretchers (bricks laid along the length of the wall), like those shown on page 217. Such designs strengthen an ordinary two-course-thick garden wall, since the headers tie the front and back courses of brick together, performing part of the function of joint reinforcement.

A TWO-COLOR PATTERN

Most large brickyards stock many different colors of brick, but to create a simple design, you can use two different colors, one for a back-ground and the other for the pattern *(page 218)*.

To plan the design, draw an outline of a full section of the wall on graph paper. Make the wall an odd number of courses high—the course that serves as a horizontal axis for the design must have an even number of courses above and below it. Find the squares that represent the center brick of the section. Fill in the pattern unit over this center brick, then fill in the rest of the section. You can now tell how many pattern units or parts of units will fit into the section and the wall, and how to begin laying the bricks.

LAYING MASONRY UNITS FOR STRENGTH

Reinforcing a brick wall

Block walls of stacked bond *(right)* need both horizontal and vertical reinforcement. The pilasters—thick columns built into the wall—bracing this wall are pairs of double-corner blocks knitted to the wall with continuous stretches of joint reinforcement laid after every second course. Steel rods run up through the cores of the blocks of each pilaster and at 4-foot intervals between pilasters; these cores are filled with grout—a mortar thinned with water for filling spaces.

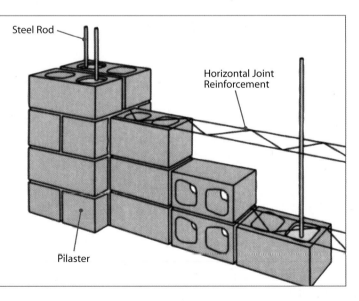

Steel Rod

Horizontal Joint Reinforcement

Pilaster

Pilaster

King Closer

Stretcher Course

Header Course

Flemish Course

Queen Closer

Strengthening a brick wall

Most traditional brick patterns are developed either from English bond *(above, left)*, in which courses of headers and stretchers alternate, or from Flemish bond *(above, right)*, which has alternating headers and stretchers in each course. Variations of these two bricklaying styles produce an enormous range of ornamental patterns, which can be heightened by using bricks of contrasting colors. In either pattern, alternate courses must

begin and end with either a quarter brick, called a queen closer, or a three-quarter brick, called a king closer. The odd sizes can be made by setting bricks more or less halfway into a pilaster or by cutting bricks. If you cut queen closers, locate them near—but not at—the end of a course. To save time, cut all the closers before you start laying bricks. Both types of wall can be braced with pilasters every 8 to 10 feet *(page 216)*.

ATTRACTIVE BLOCK WALLS

Pilaster

Half Block

Decorative walls from blocks

Standard masonry blocks can be arranged to form a number of attractive designs. Despite vertical joints that align, ordinary stretcher blocks in stacked bond *(above, left)* make a surprisingly good-looking wall. Odd sizes give you more complex patterns. A basket-weave pattern *(above, middle)* is made from units of four stretchers and a half block. Half blocks laid on their sides *(above, right)* can be arranged in a wide variety of patterns to form openings for light and air. To allow for vertical reinforcement, the blocks in all these patterns

must be laid out so the hollow cores align at least every 4 feet. Work this out on paper before pouring the footing. When you pour the footing, insert a 4-foot length of reinforcing bar into the concrete at 4-foot intervals. As you raise the wall, fit the blocks over the bar and fill the hollows with grout. For a wall taller than 4 feet, attach extra lengths of reinforcing bar with tie wire. Alternatively, add pilasters to your design every 8 to 10 feet. Install horizontal reinforcement after every second or third course.

HOW MANY BRICKS OR BLOCKS?

To determine the number of standard concrete blocks (8-by-16 inches) required for a wall, multiply the square footage of the wall by 1.125.

A typical brick wall needs 14 bricks for every square foot of wall face and 90 more for a capped 6-foot pilaster. For a two-color wall, first diagram the pattern on graph paper. Make each course one square high; let two horizontal squares represent a header and four squares a stretcher. Draw enough courses (usually two or three) to show the bond pattern, count the total number of odd-colored bricks, and multiply the figure by the number of pattern repeats you will need for the wall. Double the number of odd-colored stretchers if the pattern must show on both sides of a wall two courses thick; add the odd-colored headers and subtract the total from the number of bricks needed for the wall. Buy 5 percent extra in both colors to allow for breakage.

DESIGNING WITH COLORED BRICKS

English and Flemish variations

Bricks in contrasting colors, and courses with staggered vertical joints, give the traditional bonds shown above a different look. In English cross bond *(above, left)*, a variation of English bond, the stretcher bricks "cross," or "break joint," overlapping one another by a half brick in succeeding courses. Color emphasizes the pattern: Stretcher courses alternately comprise a single color and two contrasting colors. In Flemish spiral bond *(above, middle)*, a pattern of diagonal bands is created by the placement of dark headers. Garden wall bond *(above, right)* consists of Flemish courses in which every fourth brick is a header.

Making pattern units

The more complex designs shown above are based on pattern units of a contrasting color called eyes. The fundamental eye *(above, left)* consists of a single stretcher with headers centered above and below it. Larger eyes are formed by extending the unit by the width of one header in each course, adding headers at the top and bottom and centering the whole on the middle, or axis, course *(above, middle)*. You can expand the primary unit in this way so that it assumes a diamond shape *(above, right)*.

Combining pattern units

Large wall designs can consist of a number of pattern units defined by colored bricks and arranged in a wall symmetrically. In one widely used design *(above, left)*, eyes abut one another, forming horizontal bands. The bands are emphasized by a course of solid-color stretchers between the rows of eyes. Colored borders made of dark headers can make a simple pattern unit of light-colored bricks into a more complex design *(above, right)*.

A Brick Wall on a Block Foundation

A freestanding brick wall more than 4 feet high requires lateral support against wind and climbing children. The 8-inch-wide wall shown on the following pages is reinforced with square pilasters that measure 16 inches per side. The footings are 24 inches wide and 10 inches deep. However, specifications in your area depend on the local building code.

A CONCRETE BLOCK FOUNDATION

Regardless of the type of wall you are planning aboveground, it is most economical to build from the top of the footing up to ground level with concrete block. Buy standard "stretcher" blocks measuring 8 by 8 by 16 inches. To avoid having to cut the stretchers, you will also need half blocks measuring 8 by 8 by 8 inches. Purchase flat-ended "double-corner" blocks and "partition" blocks measuring 4 by 8 by 16 inches for the pilasters as well. A few inches below ground level, lay the masonry units for the wall itself.

SPACING PILASTERS

For ease in positioning pilasters 8 to 10 feet apart, make the length of the wall and the distance between pilasters divisible by 8 inches. Fill the cores of the blocks in the pilasters with grout. For added strength, run two lengths of reinforcing bar down through the cores of the foundation blocks in each pilaster before filling them. No. 4 to No. 8 reinforcing bar is usually required, depending on the local code. Keep in mind that a pilaster is useful as a wall support only if it is perfectly plumb.

CUTTING BRICKS

With a mason's chisel and a hammer, score a line on the brick at the point where you want it to break. Turn it over and tap the other side a few times. The brick should split on the second or third blow.

TOOLS

- Tape measure
- Chalk line
- Straightedge
- 4' level
- Torpedo level
- Shovel
- Mortar hoe
- Mason's trowel
- Mason's blocks and line
- Line pins

MATERIALS

- 1-by board for story pole
- Mortar ingredients (Portland cement, lime, masonry sand)
- Premixed grout
- Concrete blocks
- Bricks
- Truss-type horizontal joint reinforcement

SAFETY TIP

Always wear safety goggles when mixing mortar, and long sleeves and gloves when working with mortar and concrete. Wear gloves and safety goggles when cutting bricks.

BUILDING A BLOCK FOUNDATION

Center Mark

Aligning the blocks

Snap a chalk line 4 inches from the center of the footing to mark the edge of the bottom course of blocks *(above)*; snap a second line 4 inches outside the first for the edge of the pilasters. Lay a dry run of blocks for the first course, aligning them with the first chalk line. Lay a pair of blocks at the appropriate interval for each pilaster. Leave a ⅜- to ½-inch gap between the blocks to allow for mortar joints. If necessary, adjust the thickness of the joints to bring the course to the correct length. Mark the location of each pilaster on the footing with chalk.

Starting the first course

Prepare a batch of mortar. As you build the wall, spread just enough mortar for one or two blocks at a time with a mason's trowel. Lay two double-corner blocks side by side in a full mortar bed at one of the end pilaster marks. To gauge how much space to leave between the blocks, set two bricks end to end across the footing, aligning the end of one brick with the second chalk line and leaving ⅜ inch between the bricks. Lay the blocks so that their outside edges are even with the ends of the bricks (right), leaving about 1 inch between the blocks. Plumb and level the blocks with a 4-foot level. With a story pole made by marking the desired height of the blocks and the thickness of the mortar bed on a stick, check the block height. Make adjustments if necessary. Lay two more double-corner blocks for the other end pilaster, run a mason's line (photograph) between the two ends, and lay the other pilaster blocks in position. Fill the cores of the blocks with grout.

Story Pole

Double-
Corner
Block

Mortar

PREPARING MORTAR

Mortar holds masonry walls together, sealing out the elements and compensating for variations in the size of the materials. Pre-mixed bags of mortar are useful for small projects, but uneconomical for larger projects like the wall featured here.

Mortar is a mix of Portland cement, lime, sand, and water. The exact formula will vary with local conditions, particularly climate. Check with the code requirements in your area or consult local brick suppliers, masons, or contractors.

To prepare a batch of mortar, combine the dry ingredients in a wheelbarrow with a mortar hoe. Blend in the water—adding just the right amount to obtain a workable mix. To check its consistency, raise a series of ridges in the mortar with a shovel or hoe. If the ridges crumble, the mix is too dry. If they slump, there is too much water.

You can keep a batch of mortar workable for up to two hours by sprinkling water on it as needed and remixing. After two hours, prepare a new batch.

Line Pin

Stretcher Block

Line Pin

Completing the first course

Lay a stretcher block on the footing against each
end pilaster and on both sides of the other pilasters.
Center the blocks on the joint between the two
pilaster blocks and align them with the inside chalk
line. Once the mortar has begun to set, place a
line pin in each joint between the pilasters and the
stretcher blocks. Available at masonry suppliers,
the pins will anchor a mason's line to align the
remaining stretcher blocks along the footing.
Continue laying stretcher blocks (above), completing
the first course. Remove the line pins and plug the
holes they leave with mortar.

Completing the foundation

Begin the second course with a half block at each end, centering the blocks over the joints between the pilaster blocks. Check the height of the block with your story pole. Lay a corner block inside each half block, run a mason's line from one end of the wall to the other, and fill in between them with stretcher blocks. Lay partition blocks at each pilaster, sandwiching the newly laid second-course blocks *(right)*. The partition blocks must be flush with the double-corner blocks beneath them. Lay the third course as you did the first, but at each pilaster, embed a 15-inch length of truss-type joint reinforcement in the mortar across the wall before laying the blocks. Once the mortar has set, fill the openings in the blocks at each pilaster with grout so that there is a continuous column of grout from the footing up to a few inches from the top of the third course. Continuing in this manner, build the foundation to within a few inches of ground level. Check the first block you set in each new course with the story pole.

Partition Block

Half Block

Joint Reinforcement

ERECTING A BRICK WALL

End Bricks

Overhang

Making a dry run

Lay a dry run of the first course of bricks from pilaster to pilaster to check and adjust their placement. Lay the bricks in the pattern shown at left, starting with two end bricks set halfway into the core of each pilaster. Leave a gap of about ½ inch between the bricks. Lay bricks around the perimeter of each pilaster, ensuring they are flush with the outside edges of the pilasters. If the bricks project beyond the blocks, set them so the overhang is all on one side. Lay the remaining bricks of the run in pairs so their combined width equals the length of a brick *(left)*. Again, locate any overhang on one side of the foundation. Mark the location of the end bricks on the pilasters, note the gap between bricks, and remove the dry run.

Laying the leads

Start the wall by building a lead—or end structure—six courses high at each end of the wall. Spread mortar on the tops of the end pilaster blocks and along 2½ feet of the adjoining blocks. Set a 10-foot length of joint reinforcement 1 inch in from the end of the lead. Following your dry-run pattern, lay a row of bricks around the rim of the pilaster. Lay the end bricks, aligning them with the marks on the pilaster, and add three more pairs of bricks along the wall. Level and plumb each brick with a torpedo level. Set a half block in the middle of the pilaster. Begin the second course, altering the pattern so each brick is centered over a vertical joint of the course below. Stop the second course a half-brick's length from the end of the first. Start the third course, aligning the bricks with those in the first course, but make this row a full brick shorter. Set a 15-inch length of joint reinforcement across the pilaster (left), then begin three more courses of bricks, staggering the vertical joints between successive courses.

Building up the pilasters

Lay 10-foot lengths of joint reinforcement along the top of the block foundation, overlapping their ends 12 to 15 inches. At each pilaster between the ends, build six-course double leads—ones that step up from the wall on both sides as described above. To help maintain horizontal alignment, stretch a mason's line between the end pilasters. For vertical alignment, butt a straightedge against the bricks and foundation wall (right), tapping the bricks flush, as necessary. Fill the cores of the pilaster blocks with grout. Complete the courses between the pilasters, running a mason's line from line pins stuck in the vertical mortar joints next to the pilasters. Fill in the soil you dug out for the footing trench and compact it well with a tamper.

Sixth Course

Extending the wall upward

Once you have completed six courses of bricks, lay joint reinforcement along the wall. Then, build six-course leads at each pilaster. Grout the lead cores, fill in the courses between the pilasters, and repeat the process, adding joint reinforcement after every sixth course. If you laid one or two courses of brick below grade, four six-course leads will take the wall to 5 feet; an additional three courses plus a cap will take it to 6 feet.

Rowlock Brick

Capping the wall

Once the wall is 4 inches short of the desired height, lay joint reinforcement along the top, build the pilasters up three more courses, and fill in their cores. Start with a dry run of rowlocks (bricks laid on edge) along the wall between the pilasters to determine the required thickness of the remaining mortar joints. Lay the rowlocks in a mortar bed *(left)*.

Capping the pilasters

For each pilaster, cut eight 1-inch-thick pieces of brick, called closers. These serve to widen the two courses that cap the pilasters. Cut the bricks as described on page 220. Lay the first course of the cap around the rim of the pilaster with full-sized bricks; follow the basic pattern, but ensure the bricks overhang the rim by 1 inch all around. Fit closers in the gaps between the bricks. Set two bricks in the middle of the pilaster and fill the gaps with mortar. Alternating the pattern, lay the second cap course flush with the first *(right)*. Set two more bricks in the center. For the final course, center eight bricks across the pilaster.

Final Course

1" × 2¼" × 4" Closers

CHAPTER 6

The Finishing Touches

A carpet of green, punctuated by trees and shrubs, supplies almost everything needed for a well-landscaped yard. Yet a constructed element or two in the plan can make for an appealing finale. An addition as simple as a new flower bed or as ambitious as a garden pool can showcase favorite varieties or establish a fresh vantage point from which to appreciate the fruits of your landscaping labors.

Nothing perks up a landscape as quickly and noticeably as planting flowers.

Settings for Flowers or Shrubs

Clearly defined areas set aside for flowers or shrubs are part of any landscaping plan. Beds for such plantings can be dug into the ground or boldly raised above the surrounding terrain.

THE SIMPLE APPROACH

Locate ground-level beds in an area of your yard with good drainage. Apart from properly prepared soil, the only requirement for the bed is a barrier of edging to keep out grass and weeds.

Plastic edging comes in 20-foot rolls and includes a coupler for joining sections. Purchase plastic stakes separately to anchor the edging to the ground.

Aluminum edging in a choice of colors is sold in 16-foot lengths. It is molded with flanges and grooves for joining sections and comes with one anchor stake for each 4 feet of edging.

Both metal and plastic edgings bend easily, making them especially suitable for irregularly shaped beds. Right-angle couplers are also available for installing both kinds of edging around a bed with corners that are square. However, rectangular beds are also ideally suited to the mortarless brick edging shown on page 123. Whatever edging you choose for a rectangular bed, use the triangulation method to lay out square corners.

RAISED BEDS

In locations with poor drainage or crossed by large tree roots, a ground-level bed is impractical. The solution is an aboveground bed of soil framed by walls between 12 inches and 24 inches high.

Among the materials suitable for building a raised bed are stone and brick, but pressure-treated timbers are by far the easiest to work with *(page 123)*. After you have assembled the walls, fill the frame of the bed with amended soil and compost *(pages 40-41)*.

TOOLS	MATERIALS
■ Garden spade	■ Garden hose
■ Mattock	■ Stakes and string
■ Edging tool	■ Edging
■ Circular saw	■ Chalk
■ Sawhorses	■ 6-by-6 pressure-treated timbers
■ Carpenter's level	■ Mason's cord
■ Maul	■ ⅜- by 24-inch reinforcing rods
■ Electric drill	■ 10-inch galvanized spikes
■ ¼-inch and ⅜-inch auger bits	

SAFETY TIP

Gloves protect your hands during spadework. Wear a back brace to reduce the risk of injury when digging.

MAKING A GROUND-LEVEL BED

Outlining the bed

For a curved bed, lay out a garden hose in the desired shape; for a bed with straight sides, use stakes and string. Stand outside the bed and place the blade of a garden spade against the inside edge of the hose or string. Holding the shaft at a slight angle, push the blade 4 to 6 inches deep *(left)*. Cut along the outline of the bed in the same manner to make a continuous slit in the turf.

Hose

Bed Area

Preparing the bed

Working inside the bed, make a second cut 6 inches inside the first, angling the spade to remove wedges of sod from between the two cuts. Strip off the sod in the remainder of the bed with a spade or mattock *(left)*. Compost the sod, or set it aside for transplanting to another part of the yard. Prepare the soil for planting as described on page 36. Using a spade or edging tool, form the edge of the bed into a V-shaped trench about 4 inches deep *(inset)*.

EDGING CHOICES

Rim

Coupler

Plastic

Unroll the edging and lay it flat for an hour. Meanwhile, deepen the trench with a garden trowel to leave only the hose-shaped rim of the edging exposed. Bend the edging to match the trench contours and set it in place. To link edging sections, insert a plastic coupler halfway into the upper rim of one section, then slide the next section onto the coupler *(left)*. To anchor the edging, drive plastic stakes through the barb molded into the bottom. Place the point of the stake at the barb and, to assure a 45-degree angle, hold the beveled tip against the edging *(photograph)*. Position stakes at the ends of the edging, the joints, and at 4-foot intervals between them. Backfill the trench and tamp on both sides of the edging until only the rim can be seen.

Stake

Barb

Aluminum

Deepen the trench to leave ½ inch of the edging above ground level. Stand the edging alongside the bed and gently bend it to match the curves of the trench. To join lengths of edging, align the flanges at the top and bottom of one section with matching grooves in the other *(photograph)*. Push the pieces together, overlapping them at least 2 inches. To shorten the edging, increase the overlap at joints or disassemble sections for trimming with a hacksaw. Set the edging in the trench, and secure it at 4-foot intervals. To do so, hook the 12-inch aluminum stakes over the top of the edging and pound them into the ground. Backfill and tamp on both sides of the edging.

Flange

Groove

Brick

Widen the bottom of the trench with a mattock blade to a depth of about 5 inches. Tamp the trench bottom with the end of a 2-by-4. About 3 inches above the center of the trench, stretch a string between two stakes. Set a brick in one corner of the trench to prop a row of bricks set at an angle in the trench along one side of the bed. Place the bricks so that their top edges touch the string *(left)*. Brick the bed's other sides in the same fashion.

CONSTRUCTING A RAISED BED

Chalk Mark

Measuring and cutting timbers

Lay timbers to be cut across a pair of sturdy sawhorses. Mark each timber one timber-width (5½ inches for a 6-by-6) shorter than the exterior dimensions of the bed you plan to build. If the sides of the bed are more than one timber in length, plan your cutting to stagger joints from course to course. Fully extend the blade of a circular saw. Make one pass through the timber, then turn it over and make a second pass to complete the cut *(above)*.

Anchoring the base

Dig a trench 2 inches deep with a mattock or spade and lay the bottom course of timbers in the trench. With a carpenter's level, check that the timbers are level, adjusting the depth of the trench as needed to make them so. Drill ⅜-inch pilot holes for reinforcing rods, 6 to 8 inches from both ends of all four timbers. With a maul, drive a 24-inch length of ⅜-inch reinforcing rod through each hole and into the ground, marking rod locations on the fronts of the timbers in chalk.

Adding the upper courses

Lay the remaining timber courses, constructing corners as shown at right. For each course, drill a ¼-inch pilot hole, 6 inches deep, at all four corners, about 1 inch from timber center-lines. In addition, drill a hole midway along every timber and 6 to 8 inches from the end that is not in the corner. Make sure that no hole coincides with a chalk mark on the course below. Drive 10-inch galvanized spikes into the holes, then mark the spike positions with chalk on the front of all but the top course.

Spike

Chalk Mark

Decorative Wooden Containers for Plants

Wooden containers, as landscape elements, not only sustain small parcels of greenery on a deck or on a patio, but they are visually appealing in their own right. The modular design of the freestanding planter with optional benches that is shown below allows you to use your imagination to fill a space of just about any size or shape.

TREATING THE WOOD

Because the chemicals in pressure-treated wood can harm many plants, buy ordinary lumber for planters and flower boxes. Countersink the heads of all finishing nails and plug the holes with waterproof wood putty, then paint or stain the wood to seal it. Before filling a container with soil for planting, cover the bottom with galvanized screening and 1 to 2 inches of gravel.

TOOLS	MATERIALS
■ Combination square	■ 2-by-4s
■ Circular saw	■ 2-by-2s
■ Hammer	■ 2½-inch galvanized common nails
■ Plane	
■ Clamps	■ 2½-inch galvanized finishing nails
■ Saber saw	■ 2½-inch galvanized wood screws
■ Electric drill with ¹⁄₁₆-, ⅛-, and ¾- inch bits	
■ Caulk gun	■ ⅜-inch plywood for spacers
■ Backsaw and miter box	

PLANTERS WITH BENCHES

A modular system

Boxes for planting can be freestanding units or components of a larger assemblage having one or more benches. A box consists of five courses of 2-by-4s with a 2-by-2 brace in each corner and a cap of mitered 2-by-4s. These dimensions yield a planter sufficiently large for an ornamental shrub or an interesting flower arrangement, yet not too heavy to be placed on a deck. Each bench uses seven 2-by-4s, up to 8 feet long. Because the presence of benches affects box construction, plan the unit before you begin building it.

Building the base

Cut four 2-foot lengths of 2-by-4 and set them on edge to form a square. For best results, orient the end grain of the pieces as shown in the photo at right. With a ⅛-inch bit, drill two pilot holes through the face of each 2-by-4 where it overlaps the adjacent piece, then fasten each corner with 2½-inch galvanized nails. For the feet, cut two 2-by-4s, 25¾ inches long. Drill two pilot holes at each end of the feet, then lay them across the frame, about 2 inches in from the edges. Square the frame and nail the feet in place. Cut five pieces of 2-by-4, 22¼ inches long. Turn the structure over and nail the 2-by-4s to the feet as shown above, leaving uniform drainage spaces between the boards.

A JIG FOR CUTTING 2-BY-4S

For a planter that looks professionally built, it is essential that all the 2-by-4 pieces be exactly the same length. If you don't have a table saw, you can achieve the results with a circular saw and the jig shown above. A 2-by-6 at least 6 feet long serves as the base. Near one end, screw a piece of 2-by-2 to act as an end stop. A little more than 2 feet from the end stop, screw an 18-inch 2-by-2 to the base, flush against the edge, as a side stop.

Mark a 2-by-4 with a cut line 2 feet from one end, and set the board against the side and end stops. Place the blade of your saw at the cut line, then set a piece of ¾-inch plywood alongside the saw's baseplate. Put the saw aside and screw the plywood to the side stop as a saw guide. To use the jig, set your saw for a 2-inch depth. Slide a 2-by-4 against the stops, place the saw baseplate against the guide, and cut through.

Putting the box together

For the corner braces, cut four 16-inch lengths of 2-by-2. Hold a brace firmly in one corner of the base and drill ⅛-inch pilot holes through the 2-by-2 and into the 2-by-4s at the corner, offsetting the holes so they do not meet. Attach the brace with 2½-inch galvanized screws. Repeat at the other corners. Assemble the second course as you did the frame for the base, and slip it over the braces, forming the corner-joint pattern shown at left. Drill pilot holes and screw the corner braces to this course.

Finishing the box

For boxes without benches, repeat the preceding step to add the remaining three courses. However, if your plan includes benches, stop after the third course and build the fourth course as shown here—three-sided to support one bench end or two-sided to support the ends of two benches. Nail a two- or three-sided course together, as called for. Lay it on the third course, and screw the corner braces to it. Set the fifth course in place, supporting it with a scrap piece of 2-by-4 in the case of a two-sided fourth course (inset). Screw the corner braces to the fifth course. For the cap, cut four lengths of 2-by-4, 26½ inches long, then miter the ends with a backsaw and a miter box. Nail the cap pieces to the fifth course with finishing nails, set the heads, and hide the holes with waterproof wood putty.

ADDING THE BENCHES

Fitting bench slats

Place the boxes in their final locations with open sides of the fourth course facing each other. Measure the distance between the interior faces of the boxes, and cut seven 2-by-4 slats to that length. Insert the slats on edge into the space in the fourth course so that the ends are flush with the interior faces of the boxes *(above)*. Place ⅜-inch spacers—plywood works well—between the slats at both ends of the bench *(inset)*, then center the bench in the fourth course.

Spacer

Completing the fourth course

Measure the gap between the bench and the inside edge of the fourth course *(left)*, and cut a 2-by-4 filler to match. Fit the filler into the gap, then nail through the fourth course into the end of the filler to secure it. (You need not anchor the filler to the bench.) On the other side of the bench, slide a piece of 2-by-4 into the gap and against the bench. Mark a trim line on the board using the outside of the box as a guide, then cut the filler and nail it in place.

Support for Climbing Plants

Flowering or fruit-bearing plants gracefully climbing a wooden framework bring a three-dimensional touch to your landscape design. Along an exterior wall, a trellis can give plants maximum exposure to the sun, shield them from extreme weather, or provide privacy for a pool or a patio. Freestanding post-and-beam arbors control and support heavy, spreading vines like grapes and wisteria and at the same time add a touch of classic design.

THE PROPER LOCATION

Mount lightweight wood or plastic trellises at least 2 inches from the house with wooden spacers. The gap lets air circulate and helps prevent vines from attaching themselves to the wall. Erect sturdier trellises intended for bushy plants at least 6 inches from the wall.

If you want an arbor that is big enough to walk under, build it at least 4 feet wide and 7 feet high, with beams and rafters overhanging the corner posts at least 1 foot on all sides. Choose a site for the arbor that is level and use the squaring method described on page 188 to locate the corner posts.

BUILD TO LAST

Trellises and arbors must be strong enough to support mature plants in full bloom and to withstand the worst weather your region offers.

Rot-resistant redwood or cedar are excellent choices for trellises and arbors. Neither requires painting or sealing as ordinary pine does. And unlike pressure-treated lumber, they contain no preservatives harmful to some plants. No matter what material you choose, assemble the structure with corrosion-resistant galvanized nails and other hardware.

TOOLS	MATERIALS
■ Screwdriver	■ 4-by-4 posts
■ Carpenter's level	■ 2-by-4s
■ Hammer	■ 1 -by-2s, -6s, and -8s
■ Saw	■ ¼-by-2 lath
■ Spade or post-hole digger	■ Hooks and eyes
■ Adjustable wrench	■ Strap hinges
■ Stepladders	■ 6-inch carriage bolts, washers, and nuts
	■ Galvanized nails
	■ Galvanized rafter ties

TWO VARIETIES OF TRELLIS

Choosing a trellis

A simple trellis starts with a pair of 2-by-4 uprights, located parallel to a wall or at right angles to it and set at least 2 feet into the ground. A trellis to support light vines *(above, left)* begins as a rectangular frame of 2-by-4s nailed to the posts, flush with the tops. The frame should be 1 foot shorter than the height of the posts and at least 2 feet wider than the distance between them. You can weave ¼- by 2-inch lath into a uniform grid *(inset)* or buy basket weave lattice and cut it to fit the frame. For heavier vines, a grid of 1-by-2s (with the posts serving as two of the verticals) provides sturdy support *(above, right)*. Spacers that are made of 1-by-2s and sets of hooks and eyes hold the trellis 6 inches from the wall. You can cut and hinge the posts *(inset)* about 6 inches from the ground to permit tipping the trellis outward for pruning the vines or painting the house.

A POST-AND-BEAM ARBOR

Setting the posts

For each 4-by-4 corner post, dig a hole 3 feet deep with a spade or posthole digger. In soft or sandy soil, place a flat stone or brick at the bottom of each hole. Stand a post in the center of a hole with the sides aligned to the rectangular layout. While a helper uses a level to hold the post vertical *(right)*, tamp soil around the post with a 2-by-4 in successive layers a few inches deep until the hole is filled. To keep the post plumb, temporarily nail two braces to the post and to stakes in the ground. When the first post is in place, stand the other posts alongside it one at a time and mark them at the height of the first. Turn the posts over, then set and brace them in the remaining holes to the depth marked.

Spacer

Mounting the beams

Measure and cut four 1-by-8s for the beams. With a helper, lift a board even with the top of one pair of posts, the ends extending equally. Fasten the board to one post with a nail, then level the board and nail it to the other post. Mount a second on the posts' opposite sides. Drill two ½-inch holes through the boards and post, 1 inch from post and board edges *(inset)*. Insert 6-inch carriage bolts and secure with flat washers and nuts. To complete the beam, cut 7½-inch-long spacers from 4-by-4 post lumber. Nail the spacers between the boards at 12- to 18-inch intervals, flush with the top and bottom edges. Build a similar beam on the other two posts.

Installing the rafters

Measure and mark rafter positions on top of the beams at 18- to 24-inch intervals, then cut 1-by-6 boards for the rafters. Set each rafter on edge across the beams, aligned with the marks and overhanging the beams equally on each side. Toenail the rafters to the beams *(right)*, or use galvanized rafter ties *(inset)*. To prevent splits from occurring when toenailing along the edge of a board, drill pilot holes at the correct angle slightly smaller than the diameter of the nails.

Walls of Greenery from Vines

Among vines, there are eager climbers and reluctant ones. You can coax up plants such as climbing rose, which despite its name is not a natural climber, by carefully weaving their stems through a supporting trellis or by tying their stems with string or wire to a support.

However, the classic climbers are a different matter. Provided modest assistance, they will ascend a wall with little further attention. You can buy vines in flats and plant them as you would ground covers *(pages 69-70)*, or you can carefully detach established vines from their support as shown on page 243 and move them to a new location.

IVY AND BRICK WALLS

Climbing ivy and other clingers *(below)* may compromise weak mortar in a brick wall, allowing moisture to penetrate and weaken the wall's structural integrity. Perform this test: Scratch a key against the joint. If the mortar does not scrape off or crumble, your wall can support the growth.

CARING FOR CLIMBERS

Periodic pruning will keep vines bushy and robust. Climbers are generally less vulnerable to pests and disease than are low-growing plants. An occasional hosing down of the leaves helps to discourage insects. But vines are susceptible to heat scorch and drought stress from excessive evaporation from the leaves. Water them more often than low-growing varieties. Many vines tolerate frost poorly. Check with a nursery for varieties suitable to your climate.

Three ways vines hold on
Clingers, such as English ivy and Virginia creeper *(above, left)*, anchor themselves even to vertical surfaces with adhesive disks, tiny hooks, or rootlets. Moisture at anchor points can damage wood siding. Stem twiners *(center)* encircle downspouts, trellises, wires, and strings. Some, such as Hall's Japanese honeysuckle, wrap their stems counterclockwise; others, like Dutchman's pipe, twine in a clockwise direction. Tendril twiners, including plants like the sweet pea *(right)* and trumpet vine, extend threadlike spirals that wrap tightly around a thin support, such as a wire fence. Some tendril twiners also wind their stems around the support.

EASY UPKEEP FOR CLIMBERS

Thinning a climber

Prune a climbing plant in summer to improve air circulation and to permit new growth to strengthen the plant before the autumn frost. Clip and disentangle enough large stems (up to 1¼ inches in diameter) near ground level to allow light to reach all the inner branches. Prune other areas of the plant selectively, removing unhealthy stems without damaging sound ones.

Encouraging new growth

To induce lateral buds to sprout new shoots where leaves might otherwise appear, prune stems just above the buds. In general, vines that flower in the spring bloom on the previous year's growth; prune them after they bloom to give the new growth time to strengthen before winter. Those that flower in late summer or fall bloom on the current year's growth and are best pruned in late autumn when the plant is dormant or in early spring before any new growth appears.

Buds

Detaching vines from their support

When transplanting a clinger, tug gently near the adhesive disks, hooks, or rootlets that grip a wall *(above, left)*. Unravel the tendrils or unhook the leaf stalks of a twiner that attaches to a string or wire *(above, right)*. When unwinding the stems or tendrils, note whether they grow clockwise or counterclockwise, then wrap them in the appropriate direction around supports at the new location.

Tethering newly planted vines

To secure a clinging vine to a brick wall, hammer masonry nails into the mortar joints at 2-foot intervals. Loosely tie the stems of the plant to the nails with string or twist ties *(left)*. For twiners, stretch string or wire between two nails to provide vertical supports for new growth to climb. Secure the plant stem loosely to the support. Check the plant periodically, trimming back any yellowed or wilted leaves near the top. When the plant can support itself, remove the strings or ties.

Rock Gardens: Unusual Settings for Unusual Plants

A rock garden can be a handsome addition to many a landscaping plan. Featuring artfully arranged stones and uncommon plants usually found only at high altitudes, rock gardens thrive in a variety of light conditions and require little maintenance.

CHOOSING A LOCATION

Since alpine plants prefer relatively dry soil, slopes offer the best chance of success because of the superior drainage there. Choose an east-facing slope over a northern exposure, and avoid southern and western slopes; they receive too much warmth for alpine species.

A MATTER OF CHARACTER

A rock garden can mimic the geology of any area, but rather than importing stones from afar, a simpler approach is to imitate local surroundings. Flat, jagged hunks of sandstone may define the character of a rock garden design in one region; in another, granite boulders may predominate. In any case, emphasize large stones, and intersperse smaller ones among them.

The character of a rock garden depends as much on plant selection as on the kind of rock used. Choose from among the alpine varieties offered in the appendix or visit your local nursery for assistance.

HEAVY WORK

Preparing a rock garden for planting involves a fair amount of labor. Even an incline's superior drainage needs improving before you can set rocks into the slope *(opposite)*, singly or as outcrops—stacks of two or more. Tips for maneuvering heavy objects appear on page 25, but don't hesitate to contact a landscaping company to help with the largest stones.

TOOLS	MATERIALS
■ Long-handled spade	■ Large and small rocks
■ Trowel	■ Sand
■ Digging bar	■ Compost or peat
	■ Crushed stone
	■ Alpine plants, shrubs, and trees

CAUTION

Before excavating, note the location of underground obstacles such as electric, water, and sewer lines, or dry wells, septic tanks, and cesspools.

Anatomy of a rock garden

The most attractive rock gardens mimic a natural-appearing environment of rocks and plants in an aesthetically pleasing way without seeming studied or fussy. When designing the garden, consider each plant's growth habits, blooming schedule, height, and light requirements. Then, place plants in the setting you have created as they might grow in the wild.

A ROCK GARDEN ON A SLOPE

Preparing the bed

Strip the sod from the site and remove about 18 inches of soil. In the bottom of the hole, spread a 6-inch layer of rocks or broken bricks, covered by the sod, placed grass side down *(left)*. If there was no sod, cover the rocks and bricks with smaller stones or coarse sand. Mix 2 parts of coarse sand to 1 part each of the soil from the bed, compost or peat, and crushed stone. Fill the hole to ground level with the mixture.

Setting large rocks

Arrange the rocks atop the soil mixture in the desired locations. Starting at the bottom of the slope, cut a step deep enough to accommodate at least one-third the width of the first rock. Make the back of the step lower than the front so that rainwater will run toward the slope. Place the rock into the step with the long side parallel to the slope *(left)*. Pack soil mixture around the rock, filling any air pockets. Stand on the rock to test its stability. Repeat for each large rock.

Building a rock outcrop

Where an outcrop is desired, use one of the rocks set previously as a base. Select large stones that match the appearance of the base rock so that when finished the outcrop resembles a natural formation. Cover the base rock with an inch of soil and position another rock on top of it. Use a digging bar—a long metal tool helpful for gaining leverage, available at garden centers—to maneuver heavy specimens *(right)*. Repeat this process to add stones to the outcrop.

Creating Walkways for a Yard

Aesthetically, a walkway can draw the eye to a focal point in the yard. Practically, it can prevent a much trodden path from becoming a sea of mud after rain or snow. Timbered terraces or steps in a walkway not only tame modestly undulating terrain but also can protect a footpath from erosion.

STEPPING STONES

For seldom or occasionally traveled routes, flagstones, thin precast concrete slabs, or other kinds of stepping stone can make an attractive walkway. Choose elements that are 18 inches to 24 inches across. Lay rectangular slabs in pairs to form squares, as shown on page 248.

LOOSE PAVINGS

For pathways that get more frequent use, a path of pine needles, bark mulch, or gravel is more suitable. Moreover, loose paving is easier and less expensive to build with than is concrete or brick. Spreading plastic sheeting called landscaping fabric under the paving keeps weeds at bay, and an edging of bricks prevents the paving material from washing into the lawn. Make the path at least 4 feet across, wide enough for two people to walk abreast.

SAFETY TIP

Gloves protect your hands during spadework, and a back brace can reduce the risk of injury when digging. Wear goggles whenever you use a hammer.

DEALING WITH SLOPES

For gentle inclines, construct a series of terraces called ramps. Set pressure-treated 6-by-8s into the slope and spread loose paving material between them. The distance between timbers can vary from 4 feet to 10 feet; generally, the steeper the slope, the closer together the timbers should be set. Whatever the distance, keep it uniform to help reduce the risk of stumbles.

On slopes too steep for ramps, timber steps make an attractive alternative. They require a hill that allows a tread depth of 11 inches or more *(page 251)*. A steeper hill would demand an impractical amount of excavation.

Before beginning, check local building codes; in some jurisdictions, stairways of more than four steps require a handrail.

TOOLS

- Edge cutter
- Spade
- Sod cutter
- Garden rake
- Line level
- Electric drill with ½-inch bit
- 4-pound maul
- Tamper
- Sledgehammer

MATERIALS

- Stepping stones
- Sand
- Stakes and string
- Landscaping fabric
- Bricks
- Loose paving
- ½-inch steel reinforcing rods
- ⅜-inch galvanized spikes
- 6-by-6 and 6-by-8 pressure-treated timbers

A CHAIN OF STEPPING STONES

Laying out the stones

Position the stepping stones along the proposed pathway. Adjust them as necessary so that they fall naturally underfoot as you walk the path. Cut around the stones with an edge cutter *(right)*, then set the stones aside. Remove the sod with a spade, digging ½ inch deeper than the thickness of the stepping stones.

Tapping the stones down
Spread ½ inch of sand in each hole, then place the stones on the sand. Tap the stones into place with the butt of a hammer *(left)* to bring the tops level with the ground.

PATHS OF GRAVEL OR MULCH

Digging the path
Lay out a straight path with strings and stakes; for a curved path, use a rope or garden hose. Strip the sod between the marks with a sod cutter, then remove 2 or 3 inches of soil with a spade. Smooth the path with a rake. Dig edging trenches 2 inches wide and 2 inches deeper than the path. Spread landscaping fabric across the path and into the edging trenches *(right)* to curb weed growth.

Edging the path with brick

Place bricks on end in the trenches on either side *(inset)*. Pack soil behind and under the bricks as needed to align the tops just above grass level. Fill the path with loose material, then level it with a rake *(right)*.

TERRACES FOR A GENTLE SLOPE

Setting the timbers

Drill three ½-inch pilot holes through the narrow face of a 6-by-8 timber, one in the center and the others 6 inches from each end. At the bottom of the slope, dig a trench 2 inches deep and set the timber in it *(left)*. Save the displaced soil to use for fill. With a 4-pound maul, drive 24-inch reinforcing rods through the pilot holes to anchor the timber. Working up the slope, anchor a timber in a 2-inch-deep trench at each timber location.

Making the ramps

Distribute the dirt from each trench along the uphill side of the corresponding timber. Tamp the loose fill *(left)*, retaining a slight slope to the ramp to aid drainage. Uphill from each timber, spread a layer of loose paving. Keep the top of the layer below the top of the timber, and extend it up the slope to the next timber.

Loose Paving
Fill Dirt
from Trench
24" Reinforcing Rods

BUILDING TIMBER STEPS

Measuring rise and run

Drive vertical stakes at the top and bottom of the incline. Tie a string to the upper stake at ground level. Hold the string against the lower stake, and level it with a line level. Mark the lower stake at the string *(right)*, then measure the total rise, that is, the distance in inches between the mark and the ground. Divide the length of the rise by 5½ inches— the thickness of a 6-by-6 timber—to determine the number of steps. Round a fraction to the nearest whole number. Next, measure the horizontal distance between the stakes to get total run. Divide the run by the number of steps to find tread depth.

Line Level

Anchoring the first step

To make the steps, cut 6-by-6 timbers to the desired width of the stairway. Nail two timbers together with two 10-inch galvanized spikes. Nail additional timbers to one or both sides of the first two to make a step of the correct tread depth, allowing for an overlap of at least 2 inches between steps. Make as many steps as needed for the stairway. In the front timber of each step, drill three ½-inch pilot holes, one in the center and the others 6 inches from each end. Working uphill from the stake driven at the bottom of the slope in Step 1, excavate a flat area large enough for the step. Secure the step with 24-inch reinforcing rods as shown right.

Pilot Hole

Front Timber

Installing the second step

Excavate an area above the first step large enough for the second one and set it in place. With light blows from a sledgehammer *(left)*, adjust the position of the second step to the desired tread depth and step overlap. Next, drill three ½-inch pilot holes through the steps where they overlap. Drive reinforcing rods through the two steps and into the ground. Continue overlapping and securing the steps to the top of the slope.

A Pool and Water Garden

Creating a pool and water garden is a big undertaking, but the reward—a dramatic focal point for your yard and a habitat for fish and exotic plants—is substantial. Furthermore, once the pool is completed, upkeep is not any more strenuous than for a traditional flower bed.

NEW MATERIALS TO LINE THE POOL

Garden pools once were made either of one-piece rigid fiberglass or poured concrete. Nowadays the material of choice is polyvinyl chloride (PVC) plastic or a synthetic rubber called EPDM. With a life of a decade or more, these pliable membranes conform to any pool shape, from geometric to a free-form outline that is meant to mimic a natural pond.

Pool liners are available in a variety of thicknesses; 45 mils (a mil is $\frac{1}{1,000}$ inch) should be sufficient for a backyard pool. When you purchase the liner, it will come folded and boxed and is ready to set in the excavation.

CHOOSING THE PROPER SITE

Since the banks of the pool must be level all around, select a location on nearly flat terrain. To ensure sunlight for plants and fish, avoid placing the pool directly under a tree.

Some jurisdictions require a fence around pools, usually if they are more than 18 inches deep. Check your local building codes before you break ground.

FINISHING TOUCHES

To protect the liner from direct sunlight where it extends above the water line, trim the pool with a coping of flat, thin landscaping stones that overhang the edge. Unless you expect the pool area to receive heavy foot traffic, there is no need to set the stones in mortar.

A pump and fountain not only add a decorative touch to your pool but also will prevent insects from breeding on the pool's surface by keeping the water in motion. Select a fountain head and length of plastic piping in order to create the spray effect that you desire on the surface of the pool.

To power the pump, tap an electrical circuit in the house and extend it to the pool with UF (underground feeder) cable of the same gauge as that of the house circuit. Protect against shock with an outlet containing a ground-fault circuit interrupter (GFCI). Alternatively, have an electrician run a new circuit protected by a GFCI in the service panel. Or choose a solar option to avoid running cords.

FLORA AND FAUNA

Before stocking a pool, treat the water with a liquid dechlorinating agent available from pool suppliers. Since plants in containers need shallow water, either dig the pool with a 9-inch shelf around the perimeter or stand the containers on concrete blocks.

TOOLS

- Tape measure
- Powdered chalk
- Shovel
- Wheelbarrow
- Edge cutter
- Spade
- Carpenter's level
- Garden rake
- Scissors
- Push broom
- Electric drill

MATERIALS

- Ropes or hoses
- Lengths of 2-by-4
- Sand
- Pool liner
- Landscaping stones
- Dechlorinating agent
- 10-inch galvanized spikes
- UF electrical cable
- Conduit, nipple, elbow, and bushings
- LB fitting
- Metal strap
- Concrete block
- Outdoor outlet box
- GFCI receptacle

CAUTION

Before excavating, note the locations of underground obstacles—electric, water, and sewer lines, or dry wells, septic tanks, and cesspools.

Length/Width of Pool	2 x Depth of Pool	Length/Width of Liner
_____ +	_____ + 4 =	_____ feet

Calculating liner dimensions

Use the length and width of your pool in feet with the formula above to determine the size liner required. Apply the formula twice, once to find liner length and again for the width. Ignore any shelf you have planned for the pool perimeter; it does not affect the results.

EXCAVATING THE POOL

Pool Outline

Sod Line

Marking the dimensions

Outline the shape of your pool on the ground with a rope or hose. Then lay a second rope or hose 1 foot outside the first to mark the strip of sod to be removed for a stone coping. Measure across the pool outline at its longest and widest points *(left)*, then use the formula above to calculate the size of the liner you need. Squeeze powdered chalk from a chalk bottle along both markers, then lift them away.

Preparing the hole

Starting at the center of the pool outline, excavate to the desired depth—plus 2 inches for a layer of sand on the bottom. For a shelf, leave a ledge 1 foot wide about 9 inches below ground level. At the pool perimeter, slope the sides of the hole and any shelf about 20 degrees. Cut along the sod line with an edge cutter *(right)*, then remove the sod inside the line with a spade.

Shelf

Leveling the banks

Rest the ends of a 2-by-4 on opposite banks, inside the sod line. Level the board, if necessary, by removing soil from the higher bank. Mark the banks under the 2-by-4 with chalk. Leaving one end of the board on one of the marks, set the other end on the bank at a third point. Add or remove soil there to level the board, then mark that spot with chalk. Repeat this procedure to level several other points along the banks, always keeping one end of the 2-by-4 on a point that you have already leveled. Add or remove soil between these points to bring the entire bank to the same height.

Checking the depth

For a level pool bottom, mark the desired depth on a scrap of wood to use as a guide. If the pool will have a shelf, add a second mark to the depth guide 9 inches below the first. Lay a 2-by-4 across the excavation and hold the depth guide vertically against the 2-by-4 *(right)*, checking at several points for high and low spots. Use the 9-inch mark at the shelves. Add or remove soil to level the shelves and the bottom. Repeat at various points that span the hole.

Pool Depth

Shelf Depth

Preparing the bottom

Shovel sand into the hole to cushion the pool liner. With a garden rake, spread the sand across the bottom in an even layer 2 inches thick. Do not sand the shelf.

LAYING OUT A PLASTIC OR RUBBER LINER

Spreading the liner
Place the liner in the hole and begin unfolding it, working toward the banks. With a helper, contour the liner over shelves and up the sides *(left)*. Avoid overlapping folds in the liner and make sure it covers the sod line. Temporarily anchor the liner with coping stones set at several places around the edge. Fill the pool with a garden hose. Shifting anchor stones as necessary, smooth the liner so that the rising water presses it flat against the sides. Add dechlorinating agent according to the manufacturer's directions.

Securing the liner
When the pool is full, trim the liner along the sod line with a pair of scissors *(above)*. To permanently anchor the liner use a hammer to drive 10-inch galvanized spikes into the banks 4 inches inside the sod line, every 2 feet around the perimeter.

Laying the coping

Place the pump in the pool and run the power cord onto the bank where you plan to install the outlet. Spread 2 inches of damp sand between the sod line and the pool edge. Set the coping stones in the sand around the perimeter of the pool so that they extend at least 1 inch over the edge *(above)*, protecting the liner from deterioration caused by sunlight. Sweep sand into the gaps between stones with the push broom.

ELECTRICITY FOR A PUMP AND FOUNTAIN

An exit from the house

Dig a trench from your house to the receptacle location. Make the trench 6 inches deep if you plan to install rigid metal conduit for the electrical cable; otherwise make it 12 inches deep. Widen the trench near the pool to fit a concrete block. Drill a ⅞-inch hole through the house siding and floor framing to accommodate a ½-inch-diameter nipple, a short length of threaded conduit. To the back of an LB fitting, a small box used to direct cable toward the trench, screw a nipple long enough to extend into the basement or crawlspace *(above, left)*. To the other end of the LB fitting, fit a length of conduit that reaches at least 6 inches into the trench. Screw a plastic bushing to the bottom of the conduit. Push the nipple through the hole into the house and secure the conduit to the foundation with a metal strap. Inside the house, screw a bushing onto the nipple.

Making connections.

Remove the cover plate and gasket of the LB fitting. Thread UF cable up the conduit and into the LB fitting, then push it through the nipple *(above, right)*. At a convenient location inside the house, install a box for a single-pole switch. Run the UF cable to the box, then continue the circuit with indoor (NM) cable, preferably to an existing receptacle. At the switch, connect black wires to the switch terminals, white wires to each other, and ground wires to the switch and box (if it is metal) by means of jumper wires and wire caps. Replace the LB fitting's gasket and cover plate, and caulk the joint between fitting and house.

Installing the outlet box

Run cable to the end of the trench. Screw a bushing to one end of a 12-inch nipple; onto the other, thread an elbow connector. Then cut an 18-inch length of conduit; connect the threaded end to the elbow and the other end to a fitting called a threadless connector *(inset)*. Thread the cable through this assembly, set it in the trench, and lower a concrete block over it. Slip a weatherproof outlet box over the cable end and screw it to the threadless connector *(right)*. Pack soil mixed with stones around the conduit within the concrete block to prevent wobbling, then fill the trench.

Connecting a GFCI receptacle

Cover both GFCI leads marked LOAD with wire caps. Connect the black and white wires in the cable to the GFCI wires of corresponding colors marked LINE *(left)*. Attach a jumper wire to the ground screw in the box and join the jumper to cable and GFCI ground wires. Fold all the wires into the box, screw the outlet in place, and attach a weatherproof GFCI cover. In the house, turn off power to the receptacle where you intend to tap a circuit. Connect the wires in the new cable to those in the box there, black to black, white to white, and ground to ground. After screwing the receptacle to the box, restore power, and then plug in the pump.

MAINTAINING A HEALTHY POOL

Fish and plants work together to keep your pool clean and attractive. Aquatic plants provide oxygen and food for the fish, which in turn help keep the water clear by feeding on algae.

PERIODIC CLEANING

Drain your pool and scrub the liner every 3 to 4 years, or after an inch of silt has built up on the bottom. To empty the pool, lift out the plant containers, replace the fountain attachment on the pump with a hose leading outside the pool, then turn on the pump.

When about 6 inches of water remain, remove the fish with a net and place them in a clean plastic container (a new trash can works nicely) with water from the pool. Finish draining the pool, then disconnect the hose and put the pump in the fish container. Run the pump; doing so provides oxygen for the fish. Place the fish and plants in a shaded area.

Gently scrub the liner with a nylon-bristle broom, then use a wet-or-dry vacuum to suck the silt from the pool. Refill the pool and dechlorinate the water. When the pool temperature rises to within 5° of the water temperature in the container, net the fish into the pool and return plants to the shelf.

WINTERIZING A POOL

When the pool's water temperature drops to 45° F., trim plants to a height of 3 inches and move them from the shelf to the bottom of the pool.

Fish can survive the winter without food, but not without oxygen that enters the water through the surface. In regions with mild winters, water circulation from the pump may prevent the pool from freezing. Should the surface freeze over, however, you must cut in the ice an opening of at least 1 square foot. In extremely cold areas, an electric pond deicer can keep a corner of a pool ice free.

Appendix

Every grass, plant, tree, and shrub has characteristics that best suit it to one environment or another. The charts beginning on page 265, coded to appropriate climatic zone maps, highlight important factors to consider when deciding what to plant. Consult the checklist on the opposite page to schedule planting and landscape maintenance throughout the year.

Year-round Yard Care

A landscaped yard requires constant attention to stay healthy and beautiful, and each season calls for its own set of chores. Because climates vary widely in the United States, the calendar is an unreliable guide to the seasons. Changes in temperature, soil conditions, and plant appearance are more trustworthy indicators. The last hard frost marks the beginning of spring, when bulbs begin to put out shoots and perennials unfurl new leaves and stems. Rising soil temperature is a signal for preemptive weed control. Agricultural extension agencies monitor soil temperatures and can tell you other ways they affect landscaping in your area. Many flowering shrubs bloom in mid-spring, but rosebuds announce the arrival of summer. In northern climes, cooler nighttime temperatures and falling leaves signal the start of autumn. The first few killing frosts are a prelude to winter, when most plants are dormant and require little more than protection from ice and snow.

A CHECKLIST OF SEASONAL CHORES

EARLY SPRING

✔ Remove protective coverings from shrubs and plants. Remove old mulch or mix it into the soil and lay new mulch; start pruning shrubs, trees, and roses.

✔ Rake leaves from the lawn and ground covers. Reseed bare spots in the lawn, spread fertilizer, and water it. Cut grass as low as recommended *(page 50)*, and begin crab grass control by applying a pre-emergent weed-killer.

✔ Fertilize ground covers, and cut away any stringy top growth.

✔ Spray trees and shrubs with a dormant-oil spray for pest control.

MIDSPRING

✔ Cut the grass to a medium height; weed both lawn and garden weekly.

✔ When the soil is moist and easy to work, you can plant or transplant most trees and shrubs.

✔ Edge plant beds; start a vegetable garden.

LATE SPRING

✔ Prune shrubs that do not flower or that will flower in late summer or fall. Prune spring-blooming shrubs after they have lost their blossoms.

✔ Check the lawn periodically to see if the soil needs more or less water.

EARLY SUMMER

✔ Apply pesticides as needed to control fungus, insects, disease, and scale on any plants that have these afflictions. Continue spraying or dusting roses once a week until the growing season ends.

✔ If you have a pool, this is a good time to plant delicate water flowers, such as water lilies and lotuses.

MIDSUMMER

✔ Keep all plants watered well—especially any trees and shrubs planted in the spring—to prevent sun-scorched leaves.

✔ Weed flower beds and shrub beds.

✔ Cut grass about 1 inch longer than its springtime length, to prevent burnout.

LATE SUMMER

✔ Start a new lawn or renovate an old one.

✔ Examine plants for possible iron deficiency: If you see yellow leaves with dark green veins, feed the plants with an iron-rich fertilizer.

A CHECKLIST OF SEASONAL CHORES (CONTINUED)

EARLY FALL

✔ Aerate and dethatch the lawn; cut it shorter and at less frequent intervals.

✔ Dig up and move evergreen shrubs and trees or plant new ones. Wait until the leaves fall before moving deciduous plants.

✔ Plant bare-rooted roses. Water new plants regularly and mulch them lightly to deter weeds.

✔ Fall is an excellent time to start a compost pile; use yard waste such as vegetable tops, dead or dying annuals, and fallen leaves.

✔ Deep-feed tree roots.

LATE FALL

✔ Clear leaves from lawns and ground covers. Rake up pine needles and spread them as mulch for shrubs.

✔ Give roses, trees, and hedges a final pruning.

✔ Renew or replenish mulch on all shrubs. Break up any old, compacted mulch to allow air and water to reach the roots.

✔ Add dead plants from the vegetable garden to the compost pile. Spread manure or compost in the garden, then turn the soil.

✔ Until freezing temperatures set in, water plants well one morning a week to give them moisture to weather the winter.

EARLY WINTER

✔ Cover low shrubs with evergreen clippings; wrap medium-sized shrubs with burlap. Build a shelter over the plants that are near your house, to shield the branches from snow sliding off the roof.

✔ Trim hollies and other broad-leaved evergreens.

✔ Rake leaves from lawns and flower beds.

MIDWINTER

✔ Check and repair protective coverings often and, after each snowstorm, gently shake the snow from shrub branches.

✔ Take care not to shovel snow onto plants bordering walks and driveways.

✔ After bad storms, cut broken shrub and tree branches. On mild days, finish pruning trees and shrubs that flowered in the late summer and fall.

Grasses for Any Climate

This chart divides grasses into northern (cool season) and southern (warm season) varieties, each listed by common English name followed by botanical name. Details in the chart include: areas in which each grass grows best, keyed to the map on page 266; the optimal range of soil pH; the planting methods and preferred planting seasons; the amount of seed in pounds needed to sow an area of 1,000 square feet; and the ideal mowing height. The last column lists important attributes and the maintenance requirements of each variety.

Northern grasses	Zones	Soil pH	Planting	Seeding Density	Mowing Height	Characteristics
Bent grass; colonial, creeping, red top, velvet AGROSTIS	3	5.3-7.5	seed, sprig, sod in fall	1.5 -2	¾ inch	*Thick, fine texture; shiny green; grows in cool, humid climates; needs constant maintenance; water frequently, fertilize every month; dethatch yearly*
Bluegrass; Canada, Kentucky, rough-stalk POA	1-3	6.0-7.5	seed, sod in fall or early spring	2-4	2-2½- inches	*Dense, rich green, fine-textured turf; drought resistant and semidormant in warm weather; Kentucky bluegrass also grows in Zone 4*
Fescue; red, tall FESTUCA	2-5 (tall); 1-3 (red)	5.3-7.5	seed, sod in fall or early spring	6-10	2-3 inches	*Tall is tough, medium-textured turf, red is fine textured, shade tolerant; forms clumps if too sparsely sown; very low maintenance*
Ryegrass; annual, perennial LOLIUM	2-4	5.5-8.0	seed in late fall	6-8	1½-2 inches	*Fast-growing, light green annual; good for overseeding southern grasses before winter in Zones 5 and 6*
Wheatgrass; crested, western AGROPYRON	2, 4	6.0-8.5	seed in fall or early spring	1-2	2-3 inches	*Bluish green bunches; dormant in summer and tolerant of drought; avoid overwatering and overfertilizing*
Southern grasses	Zone(S)	Soil pH	Planting	Seeding Density	Mowing Height	Characteristics
Bahia grass PASPALUM	6	5.0-6.5	seed, sod in spring	4-6	2½-3 inches	*Light green, extremely coarse, drought resistant*
Bermuda grass CYNODON	4-6	5.2-7.0	seed, sprig, plug, sod in late spring or summer	2-3	½-1½ inches	*Dense, lush, quick spreading; dark green to bluish, depending on hybrid; dethatch each spring*
Blue grama grass BOUTELOUA	2, 4, 5	6.0-8.5	seed in early spring	1-2	2-2½ inches	*Drought-resistant, small, grayish leaves, which form low tufts*
Buffalo grass BUCHLOE	2, 4, 5	6.0-8.5	seed, plug, sod in spring or summer	3-6	1-2½ inches	*Rugged, slow-growing, grayish blades, which make a very smooth-textured lawn; may be left unmowed*

Kentucky Bluegrass

Western Wheatgrass

Bermuda Grass

Buffalo Grass

Zoysia

Southern, *continued*	Zones	Soil pH	Planting	Seeding Density	Mowing Height	Characteristics
Carpet grass AXONOPUS	6	4.7-7.0	seed, sprig, plug, sod in spring or early summer	1.5-2.5	1-2 inches	*Rugged, though spotty, light green turf; survives with little maintenance in acidic, sandy, and poorly drained soil and in wet locations*
Centipede grass EREMOCHLOA	4-6	4.0-6.0	seed, sprig, plug, sod in spring or early summer	4-6	2 inches	*Slow, low-growing, low-maintenance grass with yellowish, coarse leaves*
St. Augustine grass STENOTAPHRUM	6	6.0-7.0	seed, sprig, plug in spring or early summer	2-3	1-2 inches	*Coarse, dense, low-growing, bluish turf; dethatch yearly*
Zoysia **Also called Manila,** **Mascarene, Japanese,** **Korean lawn grass** ZOYSIA	2-6	5.5-7.0	seed, plug, sod in spring or early summer	2-3	½-1½-inches	*Dense, slow-growing turf, ranging from coarse grayish to fine moss green. Infrequent watering and fertilizing.*

A MAP OF GRASS ZONES

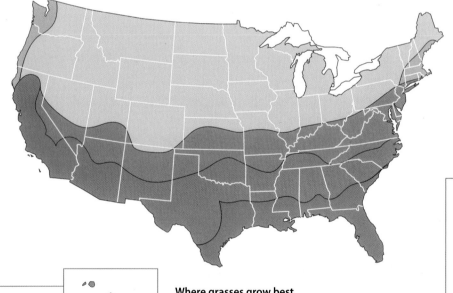

Zone 1
Zone 2
Zone 3
Zone 4
Zone 5
Zone 6

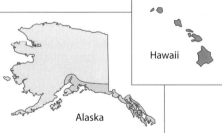

Hawaii

Alaska

Where grasses grow best

For the purpose of choosing a grass for a lawn, the United States is divided into six climatic zones. The boundaries of these regions are drawn according to environmental factors that are critical to grass health, primarily minimum winter and maximum summer temperatures and annual rainfall. Northern grasses generally do well in Zones 1 through 4; southern grasses generally prefer Zones 4, 5, and 6.

Ground Covers

This chart lists more than three dozen common ground covers by their English and Latin names, grouped according to foliage type—evergreen, deciduous, or semievergreen (plants that keep their leaves only where winters are mild). The zones in which each plant thrives, listed in the second column, are keyed to the map that appears on page 282. Semievergreen plants flourish widely but are green year round only in Zones 8 to 11. Plant height and methods of propagation are listed in the third and fourth columns. The last column notes a variety of special characteristics, such as ground covers that are well suited to slopes or rock gardens and any special light or soil requirements. All of the plants have green foliage and all flower or fruit, unless otherwise noted.

Evergreen	Zones	Height	Propagation	Special Characteristics
Bearberry ARCTOSTAPHYLOS UVA-URSI	2-11	8-16"	layering	*Good on slopes; easy maintenance; dry soil*
Candytuft, evergreen IBERIS SEMPERVIRENS	3-11	8-16"	cuttings, division	*Easy maintenance; full sun*
Carmel creeper CEANOTHUS GRISEUS HORIZONTALIS	7-11	over 16"	cuttings	*Good for slopes; full sun*
Coyote brush BACCHARIS PILULARIS	8-11	over 16"	cuttings	*Good for slopes; rapid growth; easy maintenance; full sun*
Daisy, trailing African OSTEOPERMUM FRUTICOSUM	9-11	over 16"	cuttings	*Good for slopes; rapid growth; easy maintenance; full sun; gray-green color*
Dichondra DICHONDRA REPENS	9-11	under 8"	division	*Good for rock gardens; rapid growth; easy maintenance; no flower or fruit*
Geranium, strawberry SAXIFRAGA STOLONIFERA	8-11	under 8"	division, layering	*Rapid growth; easy maintenance; moist soil; partial shade*
Grape, dwarf holly MAHONIA REPENS	5-10	over 16"	cuttings, division	*Good for slopes; rapid growth; easy maintenance; moist soil*
Heath, spring ERICA CARNEA	5-11	over 16"	division, layering	*Good for slopes; moist soil*
Heather, Scotch CALLUNA VULGARIS	4-10	over 16"	cuttings, division	*Good for slopes; easy maintenance; moist soil*
Ivy, English HEDERA HELIX	5-11	under 8"	cuttings	*Good for slopes, rock gardens; rapid growth; easy maintenance; moist soil; vine with no flower or fruit*
Juniper, Wilton carpet JUNIPERUS HORIZONTALIS WILTONII	2-11	under 8"	cuttings	*Good for slopes; easy maintenance; partial shade; no flower or fruit*

Evergreen Candytuft

Trailing African Daisy

Spring Heath

English IVY

Japanese Pachysandra

Evergreen, *continued*	Zones	Height	Propagation	Special Characteristics
Lilyturf, creeping LIRIOPE SPICATA	4-11	8-16"	division	*Easy maintenance*
Pachysandra, Japanese PACHYSANDRA TERMINALIS	4-9	8-16"	cuttings, division	*Good for slopes; rapid growth; easy maintenance; moist soil*
Periwinkle, common VINCA MINOR	4-11	under 8"	cuttings, division	*Vine that is good for slopes; rapid growth; easy maintenance; moist soil; partial shade*
Plum, Green Carpet Natal CARISSA GRANDIFLORA	10-11	8-16"	cuttings	*Moist soil*
Sandwort, moss ARENARIA VERNA STUREJA	2-11	under 8"	division	*Good for slopes; rapid growth; moist soil*
Snow-in-summer CERASTIUM TOMENTOSUM	2-11	under 8"	cuttings, division	*Good for rock gardens; rapid growth; easy maintenance; full sun; gray-green color*
Strawberry, sand FRAGARIA CHILOENSIS	8-11	8-16"	cuttings	*Rapid growth; easy maintenance; full sun*
Thrift, common ARMERIA MARITIMA	2-11	8-16"	division	*Good for rock gardens; full sun*
Thyme, wild THYMUS SERPYLLUM	3-11	under 8"	division	*Rapid growth; easy maintenance; dry soil; full sun*
Yarrow, woolly ACHILLEA TOMENTOSA	2-11	8-16"	cuttings, division	*Good for rock gardens; rapid growth; easy maintenance; dry soil; full sun; gray-green color*
Yew, spreading English TAXUS BACCATA	2-11	over 16"	cuttings, layering	*Easy maintenance; moist soil; no flower or fruit*
Deciduous	**Zones**	**Height**	**Propagation**	**Special Characteristics**
Artemesia, Silver Mound ARTEMESIA SCHMIDTIANA	3-11	8-16"	cuttings, division	*Easy maintenance; full sun; gray-green color*
Catmint, mauve NEPETA MUSSINII	4-11	8-16"	cuttings	*Rapid growth; easy maintenance; full sun; gray-green color*
Epimedium EPIMEDIUM GRANDIFLORUM	3-8	8-16"	division	*Easy maintenance; moist soil; partial shade*
Lily of the valley CONVALLARIA MAJALIS	3-7	8-16"	cuttings	*Easy maintenance; moist soil; partial shade*
Rose, Max Graf ROSA, 'MAX GRAF'	5-11	over 16"	cuttings, layering	*Easy maintenance; full sun*

Silver Mound Artemesia

Mauve Catmint

Chamomile

Mondo Grass

Moss Phlox

Deciduous, *continued*	Zones	Height	Propagation	Special Characteristics
Vetch, crown CORONILLA VARIA	3-11	over 16"	division	*Good for slopes; rapid growth; easy maintenance*
Woodruff GALIUM ODORATUM	4-11	8-16"	division	*Rapid growth; easy maintenance; moist soil; partial shade*

Semievergreen	Zones	Height	Propagation	Special Characteristics
Baby's-tears SOLEIROLIA SOLEIROLII	9-11	under 8"	cuttings, division	*Rapid growth; easy maintenance; moist soil; partial shade; no flower or fruit*
Bugleweed AJUGA REPTANS	3-11	under 8"	division	*Rapid growth; easy maintenance; moist soil*
Chamomile CHAMAEMELUM NOBILE	3-11	under 8"	division	*Easy maintenance*
Fescue, blue FESTUCA OVINA GLAUCA	3-9	under 8"	division	*Rapid growth; dry soil; full sun; no flower or fruit*
Mint, Corsican MENTHA REQUIENII	6-11	under 8"	division	*Good for rock gardens; rapid growth; moist soil; full sun*
Mondo grass OPHIOPOGON JAPONICUS	8-11	under 8"	division	*Easy maintenance; moist soil*
Phlox, moss PHLOX SUBULATA	3-9	under 8"	cuttings, division	*Good for rock gardens; rapid growth; easy maintenance; full sun*
Rose, memorial ROSA WICHURAIANA	5-11	8-16"	cuttings, layering	*Vine that is good for slopes; rapid growth; easy maintenance; full sun*
St.-John's-wort, Aaron's beard HYPERICUM CALYCINUM	6-11	8-16"	cuttings, division	*Good for slopes; rapid growth; easy maintenance*

Yard and Garden Trees

This chart lists 79 small and medium-sized ornamental trees suitable for a garden, patio, or yard; 50 are deciduous, 14 are narrow-leafed evergreens, and 15 are broad-leafed evergreens. The first column gives the common English names of each tree in alphabetical order, followed by the botanical name; the second lists the geographical zone or zones in which each tree grows best *(map, page 282)*. The third column gives the approximate height of a mature tree. Growth rates for trees vary, from less than 12 inches annually (slow), to 1 to 2 feet per year (moderate), to 3 feet or more a year (fast). Tree shapes sometimes differ within a single species, as listed in the Shape column. The Special Characteristics column includes other qualities, such as striking leaf color or unusual bark, which make trees distinctive; here, too, variations exist within a species. Also noted in this column are soil and sun requirements, and whether a tree produces flowers, fruit, or seeds. Inquire at a local nursery about trees that are native to your area; these species will flourish, because they have adapted to local conditions.

Deciduous	Zones	Height	Growth Rate	Shape	Special Characteristics
Ash, European mountain SORBUS AUCUPARIA	3-7	over 25 ft.	fast	spreading	*Full sun; flowers; fruit or seeds; colorful leaves*
Ash, Moraine FRAXINUS HOLOTRICHA 'MORAINE'	5-11	over 25 ft.	fast	columnar, rounded	*Full sun*
Bauhinia, Buddhist BAUHINIA VARIEGATA	10	to 25 ft.	fast	rounded, spreading	*Moist, acidic soil; full sun; flowers; fruit or seeds*
Birch, European white BETULA PENDULA	2-7	over 25 ft.	fast	weeping, conical	*Moist soil; full sun; colorful leaves, attractive bark*
Catalpa, common CATALPA BIGNONIOIDES	5-11	over 25 ft.	fast	rounded	*Flowers; fruit or seeds*
Cherry, double-flowered mazzard PRUNUS AVIUM PLENA	3-8	over 25 ft.	fast	conical	*Full sun; flowers*
Cherry, Higan PRUNUS SUBHIRTELLA	4-9	to 25 ft.	fast	weeping	*Full sun; flowers*
Cherry, paperbark PRUNUS SERRULA	5-6	to 25 ft.	fast	rounded	*Full sun; flowers; fruit or seeds; attractive bark*
Cherry, Yoshino PRUNUS YEDOENSIS	5-8	over 25 ft.	fast	spreading	*Full sun; flowers*
Chestnut, Chinese CASTANEA MOLLISSIMA	4-9	over 25 ft.	fast	spreading	*Acidic soil; full sun; flowers; fruit or seeds; colorful leaves*

European Mountain Ash

Common Catalpa

Yoshino Cherry

Red Jade Crab Apple

Flowering Dogwood

Deciduous, *continued*	Zones	Height	Growth Rate	Shape	Special Characteristics
Chinaberry MELIA AZEDARACH	7-11	over 25 ft.	fast	rounded	*Alkaline soil; full sun; flowers; fruit or seeds*
Crab apple, Arnold MALUS ARNOLDIANA	4-10	to 25 ft.	moderate	rounded	*Moist acidic soil; full sun; flowers; fruit or seeds*
Crab apple, Flame MALUS 'FLAME'	2-10	to 25 ft.	moderate	rounded	*Moist, acidic soil; full sun; flowers; fruit or seeds*
Crab apple, Red Jade MALUS 'RED JADE'	4-10	to 25 ft.	moderate	weeping	*Moist, acidic soil; full sun; flowers; fruit or seeds*
Dogwood, flowering CORNUS FLORIDA	5-8	to 25 ft.	moderate	rounded, weeping, spreading	*Moist, acidic soil; full sun; flowers; fruit or seeds; colorful leaves, attractive bark*
Dogwood, Kousa CORNUS KOUSA	4-8	to 25 ft.	moderate	spreading	*Moist, acidic soil; full sun; flowers; fruit or seeds; colorful leaves*
Franklinia FRANKLINIA ALATAMAHA	5-9	to 25 ft.	slow	conical	*Moist, acidic soil; full sun; flowers; colorful leaves*
Fringe tree CHIONANTHUS VIRGINICU	3-9	to 25 ft.	slow	rounded	*Moist soil; flowers; fruit or seeds; colorful leaves*
Golden-rain tree KOELREUTERIA PANICULATA	5-9	to 25 ft.	fast	rounded	*Alkaline soil; full sun; flowers*
Golden shower CASSIA FISTULA	10-11	to 25 ft.	fast	rounded	*Flowers; fruit or seeds*
Hawthorn, Toba CRATAEGUS MORDENENSIS 'TOBA'	3-10	to 25 ft.	slow	rounded	*Full sun; flowers; fruit or seeds*
Hawthorn, Washington CRATAEGUS PHAENOPYRUM	3-8	over 25 ft.	slow	conical	*Full sun; flowers; fruit or seeds; colorful leaves*
Hop hornbeam, American OSTRYA VIRGINIANA	3-9	over 25 ft.	slow	conical	*Moist soil; flowers; fruit or seeds; colorful leaves*
Hornbeam, European CARPINUS BETULUS	4-8	over 25 ft.	slow	rounded, conical	*Full sun; colorful leaves, attractive bark*
Jacaranda, sharp-leaved JACARANDA ACUTIFOLIA	10-11	over 25 ft.	fast	spreading	*Acidic soil; full sun; flowers; fruit or seeds; attractive bark*
Jerusalem thorn PARKINSONIA ACULEATA	9-11	to 25 ft.	fast	spreading	*Full sun; flowers; fruit or seeds*

Fringe Tree

Washington Hawthorn

Katsura tree

Saucer Magnolia

Japanese Maple

Deciduous, *continued*	Zones	Height	Growth Rate	Shape	Special Characteristics
Jujube ZIZIPHUS JUJUBA	6-11	to 25 ft.	moderate	spreading	*Alkaline soil; flowers; fruit or seeds*
Katsura tree CERCIDIPHYLLUM JAPONICUM	4-8	over 25 ft.	fast	spreading, conical	*Moist soil; full sun; colorful leaves*
Laburnum, Waterer LABURNUM WATERERI	5-7	to 25 ft.	moderate	rounded	*Moist soil; light shade; flowers*
Lilac, Japanese tree SYRINGA RETICULATA	3-7	to 25 ft.	moderate	spreading	*Moist soil; full sun; flowers*
Locust, Idaho ROBINIA 'IDAHO'	3-11	over 25 ft.	fast	conical	*Dry, alkaline soil; full sun; flowers*
Magnolia, saucer MAGNOLIA SOULANGIANA	4-11	to 25 ft.	moderate	spreading	*Moist, acidic soil; flowers; fruit or seeds; colorful leaves, attractive bark*
Maple, Amur ACER GINNALA	2-8	to 25 ft.	fast	rounded	*Flowers; fruit or seeds; colorful leaves*
Maple, Japanese ACER PALMATUM	5-8	to 25 ft.	slow	rounded	*Moist soil; light shade; colorful leaves*
Maple, paperbark ACER GRISEUM	4-8	to 25 ft.	slow	rounded	*Full sun; colorful leaves, attractive bark*
Maple, vine ACER CIRCINATUM	5-10	to 25 ft.	moderate	spreading	*Moist soil; light shade; flowers; fruit or seeds; colorful leaves*
Mesquite, honey PROSOPIS GLANDULOSA	8-10	over 25 ft.	fast	conical	*Dry, alkaline soil; full sun; flowers; fruit or seeds; attractive bark*
Oak, California black QUERCUS KELLOGGII	7-10	over 25 ft.	moderate	spreading	*Acidic soil; full sun; fruit or seeds; colorful leaves*
Olive, Russian ELAEAGNUS ANGUSTIFOLIA	2-7	to 25 ft.	fast	rounded	*Full sun; flowers; fruit or seeds; colorful leaves, attractive bark*
Parasol tree, Chinese FIRMIANA SIMPLEX	7-11	over 25 ft.	fast	conical	*Moist soil; full sun; flowers; fruit or seeds; attractive bark*
Pistache, Chinese PISTACIA CHINENSIS	6-9	over 25 ft.	fast	rounded	*Alkaline soil; full sun; fruit or seeds; colorful leaves*
Plum, Pissard PRUNUS CERASIFERA ATROPURPUREA	4-8	to 25 ft.	fast	rounded	*Full sun; flowers; fruit or seeds; colorful leaves*

California Black Oak

Russian Olive

Pissard Plum

Japanese Cedar

False Moss
Sawara Cypress

Deciduous, *continued*	Zones	Height	Growth Rate	Shape	Special Characteristics
Poinciana, royal DELONIX REGIA	10-11	over 25 ft.	fast	spreading	*Full sun; flowers; fruit or seeds*
Redbud, eastern CERCIS CANDENSIS	3-9	over 25 ft.	moderate	rounded, spreading	*Moist soil; flowers; fruit or seeds; colorful leaves*
Serviceberry, apple AMELANCHIER GRANDIFLORA	4-9	to 25 ft.	fast	rounded	*Moist soil; flowers; colorful leaves*
Silver bell, Carolina HALESIA CAROLINA	4-8	to 25 ft.	slow	rounded, conical	*Moist, acidic soil; flowers; colorful leaves*
Snowbell, Japanese STYRAX JAPONICUS	5-8	to 25 ft.	slow	spreading	*Moist soil; flowers; colorful leaves*
Sorrel tree OXYDENDRUM ARBOREUM	4-9	to 25 ft.	slow	conical	*Moist, acidic soil; full sun; flowers; fruit or seeds; colorful leaves*
Tallow tree, Chinese SAPIUM SEBIFERUM	7-10	over 25 ft.	fast	spreading	*Full sun; fruit or seeds; colorful leaves*
Walnut, Hinds black JUGLANS HINDSII	8-10	over 25 ft.	fast	rounded	*Full sun; fruit or seeds*

Narrow-Leaved Evergreen	Zones	Height	Growth Rate	Shape	Special Characteristics
Arborvitae, Douglas THUJA OCCIDENTALIS DOUGLASII AUREA	2-11	to 25 ft.	fast	conical	*Moist soil; full sun*
Cedar, California incense CALOCEDRS DECURRENS	5-11	over 25 ft.	fast	conical	*Moist soil; fruit or seeds; attractive bark*
Cedar, Japanese CRYPTOMERIA JAPONICA	5-11	over 25 ft.	fast	conical	*Moist, acidic soil; full sun; fruit or seeds; colorful leaves, attractive bark*
Cypress, Italian CUPRESSUS SEMPERVIRENS STRICTA	7-9	over 25 ft.	fast	conical	*Dry soil; full sun; fruit or seeds; colorful leaves*
Cypress, moss sawara, false CHAMAECYPARIS PISIFERA SQUARROSA	4-8	over 25 ft.	moderate	conical	*Moist soil; full sun*
Fir, China CUNNINGHAMIA LANCEOLATA	6-9	to 25 ft.	fast	conical	*Acidic soil; fruit or seeds; colorful leaves, attractive bark*
Juniper, blue column JUNIPERUS CHINENSIS COLUMNARIS	3-9	to 25 ft.	moderate	conical	*Dry soil; full sun*
Pine, Japanese black PINUS THUNBERGIANA	5-11	over 25 ft.	fast	spreading, conical	*Dry soil; full sun; fruit or seeds*

Japanese Black Pine

English Holly

Oleander

Sweet Orange

Pineapple Guava

Narrow-Leaved, *continued*	Zones	Height	Growth Rate	Shape	Special Characteristics
Pine, Norfolk Island ARAUCCARIA HETEROPHYLLA	7-11	over 25 ft.	fast	conical	*Moist, acidic soil; full sun; fruit or seeds*
Pine, Tanyosho PINUS DENSIFLORA UMBRACULIFERA	3-7	to 25 ft.	slow	spreading	*Dry soil; full sun; fruit or seeds; colorful leaves*
Pine, umbrella SCIADOPITYS VERTICILLATA	4-11	to 25 ft.	slow	conical	*Moist, alkaline soil; full sun; fruit or seeds*
Podocarpus yew PRODOCARPUS MACROPHYLLUS	8-11	to 25 ft.	moderate	columnar	*Moist soil; light shade; colorful leaves*
Spruce, Serbian PICEA OMORIKA	4-7	over 25 ft.	slow	conical	*Full sun; fruit or seeds*
Yew, Irish TAXUS BACCATA STRICTA	5-11	to 25 ft.	slow	columnar, conical	*Acidic soil; fruit or seeds; colorful leaves*
Broad-Leaved Evergreen	Zones	Height	Growth Rate	Shape	Special Characteristics
Ash, shamel FRAXINUS UHDEI 'MAJESTIC BEAUTY'	9-11	over 25 ft.	fast	spreading	*Moist, alkaline soil; full sun*
Camphor tree CINNAMOMUM CAMPHORA	9-11	over 25 ft.	moderate	spreading	*Flowers; fruit or seeds; colorful leaves*
Cootamundra wattle ACACIA BAILEYANA	10-11	to 25 ft.	fast	rounded	*Dry soil; full sun; flowers; colorful leaves*
Elm, Chinese ULMUS PARVIFOLIA	4-11	over 25 ft.	fast	weeping	*Full sun*
Holly, English ILEX AQUIFOLIUM	6-10	over 25 ft.	slow	rounded	*Acidic soil; full sun; fruit or seeds; colorful leaves*
Horsetail beefwood CASUARINA EQUISETIFOLIA	9-11	over 25 ft.	fast	conical	*Fruit or seeds*
Laurel LAURUS NOBILIS	6-11	to 25 ft.	slow	conical	*Fruit or seeds*
Loquat ERIOBOTRYA JAPONICA	8-11	to 25 ft.	fast	spreading	*Moist soil; flowers; fruit or seeds; colorful leaves*
Oleander NERIUM OLEANDER	8-11	to 25 ft.	moderate	rounded	*Moist soil; full sun; flowers*
Olive, common OLEA EUROPAEA	9-11	to 25 ft.	moderate	rounded	*Dry soil; full sun; flowers; fruit or seeds; attractive bark*
Orange, sweet CITRUS SINENSIS	9-11	to 25 ft.	moderate	rounded	*Moist soil; full sun; flowers; fruit or seeds*
Osmanthus, holly OSMANTHUS HETEROPHYLLUS	7-11	to 25 ft.	fast	rounded	*Dry soil; light shade; flowers*
Pepper tree, California SCHINUS MOLLE	9-11	over 25 ft.	moderate	weeping	*Full sun; flowers; fruit or seeds*
Photinia, Fraser PHOTINIA FRASERI	8-11	to 25 ft.	moderate	spreading	*Flowers; fruit or seeds; colorful leaves*
Pineapple guava FEIJOA SELLOWIANA	8-11	to 25 ft.	fast	rounded	*Moist soil; flowers; fruit or seeds; colorful leaves*

Garden Shrubs

This chart lists 58 flowering shrubs by their common English names, followed by their botanical names. The numbered zones in which each shrub can be grown are keyed to the map on page 282. In the chart's third column the approximate height for each variety is listed. Colored circles in the fourth column indicate the range of flower colors usually produced by

each shrub or its relatives. To the right of the colors is the shrub's blooming season. The Special Characteristics column contains uses to which the plant is well suited—a hedge or a ground cover, for example; its soil and sun preferences; and the presence of fruit, attractive foliage, or a pleasant fragrance.

Flowering	Zones	Height	Flower Colors	Blooming Season	Special Characteristics
Acacia, rose ROBINIA HISPIDA	5-9	to 6 ft.	●●	spring-summer	*Ground cover; full sun*
Almond, flowering PRUNUS TRILOBA	5-9	over 6 ft.	●●	spring	*Full sun; fruit; attractive foliage*
Azalea, catawba RHODODENDRON CATAWBIENSE	3-10	over 6 ft.	●●●●	spring	*Moist, acidic soil; shade*
Azalea, Exbury hybrid RHODODENDRON	5-8	to 6 ft.	○●●●●	summer	*Moist, acidic soil; attractive foliage*
Azalea, flame RHODODENDRON CALENDULACEUM	4-10	to 6 ft.	○●●●	summer	*Moist, acidic soil*
Azalea, pinxter-bloom RHODODENDRON NUDIFLORUM	3-8	to 6 ft.	○●●	spring	*Moist, acidic soil*
Barberry, Japanese BERBERIS THUNBERGII	4-10	over 6 ft.	○○	spring	*Hedge; fruit*
Barberry, Mentor BERBERIS MENTORENSIS	5-10	over 6 ft.	○○	spring	*Hedge; fruit*
Beauty-bush KOLKWITZIA AMBILIS	4-9	over 6 ft.	●●	spring	*Fruit; attractive foliage*
Broom, hybrid CYTISUS HYBRIDS	6-11	any	○○○●●●●	spring	*Full sun; fragrant*

Exbury Hybrid Azalea

Japanese Barberry

Hybrid Broom

Cornelian Cherry

Bush Cinquefoil

Flowering, *continued*	Zones	Height	Flower Colors	Blooming Season	Special Characteristics
Buckeye, bottlebrush AESCULUS PARVIFLORA	4-10	over 6 ft.	○	summer	*Attractive foliage*
Butterfly bush, fountain BUDDLEIA ALTERNIFOLIA	5-11	over 6 ft.	●●	spring-summer	*Full sun; attractive foliage; fragrant*
Cherry, Cornelian CORNUS MAS	4-8	over 6 ft.	○○	spring	*Fruit; attractive foliage*
Cherry, western sand PRUNUS BESSEYI	3-6	over 6 ft.	○	spring	*Full sun; fruit*
Chokeberry, black ARONIA MELANOCARPA	4-10	under 3 ft.	○●●	spring	*Fruit; attractive foliage*
Chokeberry, brilliant ARONIA ARBUTIFOLIA BRILLIANTISSIMA	4-10	over 6 ft.	○●●	spring	*Fruit; attractive foliage*
Cinquefoil, bush POTENTILLA FRUTICOSA	2-9	to 6 ft.	○○○	summer-fall	*Full sun*
Cotoneaster, early COTONEASTER ADPRESSUS	4-11	under 3 ft.	●●	summer	*Full sun; fruit; attractive foliage*
Cotoneaster, horizontal COTONEASTER HORIZONTALIS	5-11	under 3 ft.	●●●●	summer	*Ground cover; full sun; attractive foliage*
Cotoneaster, Sungari COTONEASTER RACEMIFLORUS	3-11	over 6 ft.	○	summer	*Full sun; fruit; attractive foliage*
Crape myrtle LAGERSTROEMIA INDICA	7-10	over 6 ft.	○●●●●	summer	*Hedge; moist soil; full sun; attractive foliage*
Daphne, February DAPHNE MEZEREUM	4-9	under 3 ft.	●●	spring	*Fruit; fragrant*
Deutzia, slender DEUTZIA GRACILIS	4-9	to 6 ft.	○	spring	*Hedge*
Enkianthus, redvein ENKIANTHUS CAMPANULATUS	4-9	over 6 ft.	○	spring	*Moist, acidic soil; attractive foliage*
Forsythia, border FORSYTHIA INTERMEDIA	5-9	over 6 ft.	○○	spring	*Hedge*
Hazelnut, curly CORYLUS AVELLANA CONTORTA	4-9	over 6 ft.	○○	spring	*Attractive foliage*

Horizontal Cotoneaster

Crape Myrtle

Kerria

Common Lilac

Lemoine Mock Orange

Flowering, *continued*	Zones	Height	Flower Colors	Blooming Season	Special Characteristics
Honeysuckle, Amur LONICERA MAACKII	2-9	over 6 ft.	○	spring	*Fruit; fragrant*
Honeysuckle, Tatarian LONICERA TATARICA	3-9	over 6 ft.	○●●	spring	*Fruit*
Honeysuckle, winter LONICERA FRAGRANTISSIMA	5-9	to 6 ft.	○	spring	*Fruit; fragrant*
Hydrangea, peegee HYDRANGEA PANCULATA	4-9	over 6 ft.	○●●	summer-fall	*Moist soil*
Jasmine, winter JASMINUM NUDIFLORUM	6-9	over 6 ft.	○○	spring	*Full sun*
Kerria KERRIA JAPONICA	4-9	to 6 ft.	○○	spring-summer-fall	*Attractive foliage*
Lilac, common SYRINGA VULGARIS	3-7	over 6 ft.	○○○●●●●	spring	*Fragrant*
Mock orange, Lemoine PHILADELPHUS LEMOINEI	5-9	to 6 ft.	○	summer	*Fragrant*
Olive, Russian ELAEAGNUS ANGUSTIFOLIA	2-9	over 6 ft.	○○	summer	*Hedge; full sun; fruit; attractive foliage; fragrant*
Pearlbush, common EXOCHORDA RACEMOSA	5-9	over 6 ft.	○	spring	*Full sun*
Photinia, Oriental PHOTINIA VILLOSA	4-8	over 6 ft.	○	spring	*Fruit; attractive foliage*
Plum, beach PRUNUS MARITIMA	3-7	to 6 ft.	○	spring	*Full sun; fruit*
Privet, Amur LIGUSTRUM AMURENSE	3-9	over 6 ft.	○	summer	*Hedge; fruit*
Privet, Regel LIGUSTRUM OBTUSIFOLIUM	3-9	to 6 ft.	○	summer	*Hedge; fruit*
Privet, vicary golden LIGUSTRUM VICARYI	4-9	over 6 ft.	○	summer	*Hedge; fruit; attractive foliage*

Pussy Willow

Hybrid Flowering Quince

Marie's Double File Viburnum

Hybrid Weigela

Chinese Witch Hazel

Flowering, *continued*	Zones	Height	Flower Colors	Blooming Season	Special Characteristics
Pussy willow SALIX DISCOLOR	2-9	over 6 ft.	○	spring	*Moist soil; full sun*
Quince, hybrid flowering CHAENOMELES HYBRIDS	6-10	to 6 ft.	○●●	spring	*Hedge; full sun*
Rose, Japanese ROSA RUGOSA	2-10	to 6 ft.	○●●	summer-fall	*Full sun; fruit; attractive foliage; fragrant*
Snowberry SYMPHORICARPOS ALBUS	3-9	to 6 ft.	●●	summer	*Hedge; fruit*
Spirea, bridal-wreath SPIRAEA PRUNIFOLIA	4-10	over 6 ft.	○	spring	*Hedge; attractive foliage*
Spirea, Bumalda SPIRAEA BUMALDA	5-10	under 3 ft.	●●	summer	*Attractive foliage*
Spirea, Ural false SORBARIA SORBIFOLIA	2-8	to 6 ft.	○	summer	*Moist soil*
Spirea, Vanhoutte SPIRAEA VANHOUTTEI	4-10	to 6 ft.	○	spring	*Hedge*
Summer-sweet CLETHRA ALNIFOLIA	3-10	to 6 ft.	○	summer	*Moist, acidic soil; attractive foliage; fragrant*
Sweet shrub CALYCANTHUS FLORIDUS	4-10	to 6 ft.	●●	spring	*Moist soil; attractive foliage; fragrant*
Tamarisk, five-stamened TAMARIX PENTANDRA	2-11	over 6 ft.	●●	summer	*Sun; attractive foliage*
Viburnum, fragrant snowball VIBURNUM CARLCEPHALUM	5-9	over 6 ft.	○	spring	*Hedge; fruit; attractive foliage; fragrant*
Viburnum, Marie's double file VIBURNUM PLICATUM	5-9	over 6 ft.	○	spring	*Hedge; fruit; attractive foliage*
Viburnum, Siebold VIBURNUM SIEBOLDII	4-9	over 6 ft.	○	spring	*Fruit; attractive foliage*
Weigela, hybrid WEIGELA	5-9	to 6 ft.	○●●	spring	
Winter hazel, fragrant CORYLOPSIS GLABRESCENS	5-9	over 6 ft.	○○	spring	*Moist, acidic soil; attractive foliage; fragrant*
Witch hazel, Chinese HAMAMELIS MOLLIS	5-9	over 6 ft.	○○	spring	*Moist soil; attractive foliage; fragrant*

This chart lists 20 evergreen shrubs by their common names, then by their botanical names. The numbered zones in which each shrub can be grown refer to the map on page 282. Special characteristics and growing conditions are mentioned in the last column; these include specific uses, such as a lawn specimen, hedge, screen, or ground cover; soil requirement; and whether the plant produces fruit, berries, or flowers.

Evergreen	Zones	Height	Foliage Color	Special Characteristics
Arbor vitae, Berckman's golden PLATYCLADUS ORIENTALIS	7-11	to 6 ft.	green, yellow-green	*Hedge, screen; moist soil*
Bearberry, 'Point Reyes' ARCTOSTAPHYLOS UVA-URSI 'POINT REYES'	2-11	under 1 ft.	dark green	*Ground cover; dry, acidic soil; fruits or berries; pink-red flowers*
Box, edging BUXUS SEMPERVIRENS SUFFRUTICOSA	5-6	to 3 ft.	blue-green	*Lawn specimen; hedge; moist soil*
Camellia, common CAMELLIA JAPONICA	7-11	to 10 ft.	dark green	*Lawn specimen, hedge; moist, acidic soil; pink-red flowers*
Cypress, false slender hinoki CHAMAECYPARIS OBTUSA	4-8	to 6 ft.	dark green	*Lawn specimen; moist soil*
Cypress, false thread sawara CHAMAECYPARIS PISIFERA	4-8	to 10 ft.	green	*Lawn specimen; moist soil*
Fire thorn, Laland PYRACANTHA COCCINEA	5-11	to 10 ft.	dark green	*Hedge; fruits or berries; white flowers*
Grape, Oregon holly MAHONIA AQUIFOLIUM	4-8	to 6 ft.	green	*Fruits or berries; yellow-orange flowers*
Holly, American ILEX OPACA	5-9	to 10 ft.	green	*Hedge; acidic soil; fruits or berries*
Holly, Burford ILEX CORNUTA	6-9	to 10 ft.	green	*Hedge; acidic soil; fruits or berries*
Holly, Japanese ILEX CRENATA	5-7	to 10 ft.	dark green	*Hedge; acidic soil; fruits or berries*
Juniper, Gold Coast JUNIPERUS CHINENSIS AUREA	3-11	to 3 ft.	yellow-green	*Lawn specimen, ground cover*
Juniper, tamarix JUNIPERUS SABINA	3-11	to 3 ft.	blue-green	*Ground cover*

Laland Fire Thorn

Gold Coast Juniper

Mountain Laurel

Dwarf Alberta Spruce

Tea Tree

Evergreen, *continued*	Zones	Height	Foliage Color	Special Characteristics
Juniper, Wilton carpet JUNIPERUS HORIZONTALIS	3-11	under 1 ft.	blue-green	*Ground cover*
Laurel, mountain KALMIA LATIFOLIA	4-9	to 10 ft.	dark green	*Lawn specimen; moist, acidic soil; pink-red flowers*
Nandina NANDINA DOMESTICA	6-11	to 6 ft.	green	*Moist soil; fruits or berries; white flowers*
Pine, Mugo PINUS MUGO	2-8	to 3 ft.	dark green	*Lawn specimen, hedge, ground cover*
Spruce, dwarf Alberta PICEA GLAUCA	2-6	to 10 ft.	blue-green	*Lawn specimen, hedge, screen*
Tea tree LEPTOSPERMUM SCOPARIUM	9-11	to 10 ft.	green	*Hedge; acidic soil; pink-red flowers*
Yew, spreading English TAXUS BACCATA REPANDENS	5-11	to 6 ft.	dark green	*Lawn specimen, hedge; acidic soil*

Plants for Rock Gardens

In the chart below, plants are listed by their most common English names, followed by their scientific Latin names. The second column indicates the climatic zone or zones in which each plant can be grown, keyed by number to the map on page 282. All of the plants flower, and a few plants have additional special traits. Bishop's hat, fringed bleeding heart, and leadwort have distinctive foliage, while common thrift is an evergreen. Plant heights, listed in the next column, include the height of the flowers, and the fourth column indicates the blossoms' range of colors. The Growth Habit column shows that most of these plants grow upright, but some grow either by spreading or by trailing from a central stem. Special soil and light conditions in which specific plants thrive appear in the last column.

Flowering	Zones	Height	Flower Colors	Growth Habit	Soil and Light
Anemone, European wood ANEMONE NEMOROSA	3-8	under 6"	○◐●●●●	upright	*acidic soil; partial shade*
Basket-of-gold AURINIA SAXATILIS	4	6-12"	◐◐	spreading	*full sun*
Bishop's hat EPIMEDIUM GRANDIFLORUM	3-8	6-12"	○◐○◐●●●●	upright	*shade*
Bleeding heart, fringed DICENTRA EXIMIA	3-8	over 12"	○◐●●	upright	*acidic soil; shade*
Candytuft, evergreen IBERIS SEMPERVIRENS	3-11	6-12"	○◐	spreading	*alkaline soil; full sun*
Cheddar plant DIANTHUS GRATIANOPOLITANUS	4	6-12"	○◐●●	upright	*full sun*
Foamflower TIARELLA CORDIFOLIA	4	6-12"	○◐	upright	*acidic soil; shade*

Flowering, *continued*	Zones	Height	Flower Colors	Growth Habit	Soil and Light
Goldenstar CHRYSOGONUM VIRGINIANUM	4-8	6-12"	◐◐	upright, spreading	*acidic soil; shade*
Harebell, Carpathian CAMPANULA CARPATICA	3-8	6-12"	○◐◐●	upright	*full sun*
Iris, dwarf bearded IRIS PUMILA	5	6-12"	○◐◐◐◐●●●	upright	*alkaline soil; full sun*
Iris, dwarf crested IRIS CRISTATA	3-8	under 6"	○◐●●	upright	*acidic soil; partial shade*
Leadwort CERATOSTIGMA PLUMBAGINOIDES	6-11	under 6"	◐●	spreading	*partial shade*
Phlox, wild blue PHLOX DIVARICATA	4	6-12"	○◐●●	spreading	*acidic soil; partial shade*
Pink, wild SILENE CAROLINIANA	6	6-12"	◐●	upright	*partial shade*
Primrose, Siebold PRIMULA SIEBOLDII	5	6-12"	○◐◐●●●	upright	*acidic soil; partial shade*
Rose, sun HELIANTHEMUM NUMMULARIUM	5-9	6-12"	○◐◐◐◐●	upright, trailing	*alkaline soil; full sun*
Sandwort, mountain ARENARIA MONTANA	4-11	under 6"	○◐	trailing	*acidic soil; full sun*
Soapwort, rock SAPONARIA OCYMOIDES	2-8	6-12"	○◐●●	trailing	*full sun*
Thrift, common ARMERIA MARITIMA	4-8	6-12"	○◐●●	upright	*full sun*

European Wood Anemone   Basket-of-Gold   Evergreen Candytuft   Goldenstar   Dwarf Bearded Iris

A Map of Minimum Temperatures

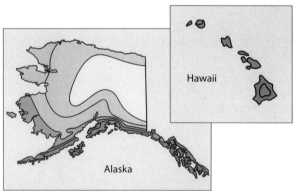

Hawaii

Alaska

Zone 1	Below -50° F.
Zone 2	-50° to -40°
Zone 3	-40° to -30°
Zone 4	-30° to -20°
Zone 5	-20° to -10°
Zone 6	-10° to -0°
Zone 7	0° to 10°
Zone 8	10° to 20°
Zone 9	20° to 30°
Zone 10	30° to 40°
Zone 11	Above 40°

Plants and winter cold

Successful landscaping depends upon a choice of plants that thrive on the land they adorn. Since soil conditions and moisture levels can usually be altered artificially, limitations on where plants will flourish depend largely upon the severity of winter cold. This map devised by the U.S. Department of Agriculture divides the United States into 11 numbered and colored zones, each distinguished by an average minimum winter temperature. Use the charts of ground covers *(pages 267-269)*, flowering shrubs *(pages 275-278)*, and rock-garden plants *(page 280)* with this map to select plants that will grow best in your area.

Index

Index

Index

More Great Books from Fox Chapel Publishing